Houghton Mifflin Harcourt

GRADE 8

Common Core Assessment Readiness

Contents

Analyze and solve linear equations and pairs of simultaneous linear equations.

8.EE.7 Solve linear equations in one variable.

8.EE.8 Analyze and solve pairs of simultaneous linear equations.

Functions

Define, evaluate, and compare functions.

Use functions to model relationships between quantities.

Geometry

Understand congruence and similarity using physical models, transparencies, or geometry software.

Understand and apply the Pythagorean Theorem.

Solve real-world and mathematical problems involving volume of cylinders, cones, and spheres.

Statistics and Probability

Investigate patterns of association in bivariate data.

8.SP.2	Know that straight lines are widely used to model relationships between two quantitative variables. For scatter plots that suggest a linear association, informally fit a straight line, and informally assess the model fit by judging the closeness of the data points to the line.	61
8.SP.3	Use the equation of a linear model to solve problems in the context of bivariate measurement data, interpreting the slope and intercept.	63
8.SP.4	Understand that patterns of association can also be seen in bivariate categorical data by displaying frequencies and relative frequencies in a two-way table. Construct and interpret a two-way table summarizing data on two categorical variables collected from the same subjects. Use relative frequencies calculated for rows or columns to describe possible association between the two variables.	65

Some of the assessment items for the Standards for Mathematical Content cited in the preceding Contents also involve one or more of the following Standards for Mathematical Practice.

Standards for Mathematical Practice

MP.1	Make sense of problems and persevere in solving them.
MP.2	Reason abstractly and quantitatively.
MP.3	Construct viable arguments and critique the reasoning of others.
MP.4	Model with mathematics.
MP.5	Use appropriate tools strategically.
MP.6	Attend to precision.
MP.7	Look for and make use of structure.
MP.8	Look for and express regularity in repeated reasoning.

8.NS.1

SELECTED RESPONSE

Select the correct answer.

1. What is the decimal equivalent of the rational number $-\frac{1}{8}$?

   Ⓐ −0.125   Ⓒ −1.8

   Ⓑ −1.25   Ⓓ −12.5

2. What is the decimal equivalent of the rational number $\frac{6}{11}$?

   Ⓐ 0.54   Ⓒ $0.\overline{54}$

   Ⓑ $0.5\overline{4}$ Ⓓ $1.8\overline{3}$

3. What rational number has −0.875 as its decimal equivalent?

   Ⓐ $-\frac{7}{80}$ Ⓒ $-\frac{7}{8}$

   Ⓑ $-\frac{4}{5}$ Ⓓ $-\frac{35}{4}$

4. Pierre worked $5\frac{3}{8}$ hours today. What is the decimal equivalent of $5\frac{3}{8}$?

   Ⓐ 5.25   Ⓒ $5.37\overline{5}$

   Ⓑ $5.\overline{3}$ Ⓓ 5.625

Select all correct answers.

5. A company can hire 99 new employees. There are 243 applicants. Which of the following rational numbers represent the ratio of applicants to available positions?

   Ⓐ 2.45   Ⓓ $\frac{11}{27}$

   Ⓑ $2.4\overline{5}$ Ⓔ $\frac{27}{11}$

   Ⓒ $2.\overline{45}$ Ⓕ $2\frac{5}{11}$

6. Which rational numbers fall between 2.7 and 2.8 on a number line?

   Ⓐ $\frac{11}{4}$ Ⓓ $2\frac{41}{50}$

   Ⓑ $2\frac{19}{25}$ Ⓔ $\frac{277}{100}$

   Ⓒ $\frac{21}{8}$ Ⓕ $2\frac{5}{6}$

Match each rational number with its decimal equivalent.

____ 7. $-\frac{41}{33}$ A −1.024

____ 8. $-\frac{112}{90}$ B $-1.02\overline{4}$

                        C −1.204

____ 9. $-\frac{31}{25}$ D −1.24

____ 10. $-\frac{338}{330}$ E $-1.2\overline{4}$

                        F $-1.\overline{24}$

____ 11. $-\frac{128}{125}$

CONSTRUCTED RESPONSE

12. On a final exam, Alex answered 21 out of 25 questions correctly. He needs to score at least 80% to receive a B in the course.

    a. Written as a decimal, what portion of Alex's answers were correct?

    _____

    b. How many questions need to be answered correctly to receive a score of 80%? Show your work.

    _____

    _____

    c. Did Alex score at least 80% on his final exam? Give two reasons why.

    _____

    _____

13. Does 0.010110111011110… represent a rational number or an irrational number? Explain your reasoning.

_____

_____

_____

_____

14. A local middle school has 99 computers and 333 students. What is the number of students per computer at the school? Write your answer as both a rational number in simplest form and a decimal.

_____

_____

15. What rational number has $0.3\overline{4}$ as its decimal equivalent? Show your work.

_____

_____

_____

_____

_____

_____

16. Sometimes the rational number $\frac{22}{7}$ is used as an approximation of the irrational number π, whose decimal form is 3.14159…, which neither terminates nor repeats. To how many decimal places does the decimal form of $\frac{22}{7}$ agree with the decimal form of π?

_____

_____

_____

17. Let n be the decimal form of a rational number $\frac{a}{b}$, where a and b are nonzero integers.

   a. If n is a terminating decimal, what is true about the factors of b? Explain.

   _____

   _____

   b. If n is a repeating decimal, what can be said about the number of digits in the repeating block? Explain.

   _____

   _____

18. Write the decimal equivalents of $\frac{1}{11}$, $\frac{2}{11}$, and $\frac{3}{11}$. Then use the results to predict the decimal equivalent of $\frac{9}{11}$.

   _____

   _____

   _____

19. On a recent math test Marcos was asked to find the decimal equivalent of $\frac{22}{25}$. Marcos gave the answer $\frac{22}{25} = 1.\overline{136}$.

   a. Find the decimal equivalent of $\frac{22}{25}$ and decide whether Marcos gave a correct or incorrect answer.

   _____

   _____

   b. What mistake did Marcos most likely make, if any?

   _____

   _____

8.NS.2

SELECTED RESPONSE
Select the correct answer.

1. Between which pair of decimals does $\sqrt{13}$ fall on a number line?

   Ⓐ Between 3.2 and 3.3

   Ⓑ Between 3.4 and 3.5

   Ⓒ Between 3.6 and 3.7

   Ⓓ Between 3.8 and 3.9

2. The number e is an irrational number approximately equal to 2.718. Between which pair of square roots does e fall?

   Ⓐ $\sqrt{2}$ and $\sqrt{3}$ Ⓒ $\sqrt{7}$ and $\sqrt{8}$

   Ⓑ $\sqrt{5}$ and $\sqrt{6}$ Ⓓ $\sqrt{10}$ and $\sqrt{11}$

3. To the nearest tenth, what is the value of $\left(\sqrt{2}\right)^3$?

   Ⓐ 1.3   Ⓒ 2.7

   Ⓑ 2.4   Ⓓ 2.8

Select all correct answers.

4. Which of the following numbers fall between 4.7 and 4.8 on a number line?

   Ⓐ $\sqrt{22}$ Ⓓ $1+\sqrt{15}$

   Ⓑ 1.5π Ⓔ $2\sqrt{6}$

   Ⓒ $\dfrac{\sqrt{91}}{2}$ Ⓕ $5-\pi$

5. Suppose each irrational number below is approximated by the whole number to which it is closest. Which of the irrational numbers have whole number approximations that are even?

   Ⓐ $2\sqrt{32}$ Ⓓ $\sqrt{52}-3$

   Ⓑ $5+\sqrt{18}$ Ⓔ $3\sqrt{14}$

   Ⓒ $\sqrt{24}$ Ⓕ $\sqrt{20}+\sqrt{26}$

Select the correct answer for each lettered part.

6. Determine whether each number is greater than $\sqrt{10}$.

   a. $\sqrt{3}+\sqrt{6}$ ○ Yes ○ No

   b. $2\sqrt{3}$ ○ Yes ○ No

   c. $\dfrac{\sqrt{22}}{2}$ ○ Yes ○ No

   d. $\sqrt{14}-\sqrt{3}$ ○ Yes ○ No

   e. $\sqrt{\sqrt{10}}$ ○ Yes ○ No

CONSTRUCTED RESPONSE

7. On the coordinate grid shown below, consecutive grid lines are 1 cm apart. Find the perimeter of quadrilateral *ABCD* to the nearest 0.1 cm. Show your work and explain your reasoning.

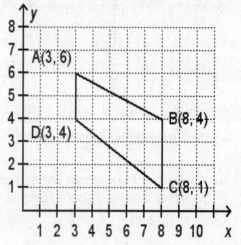

_____

_____

_____

_____

_____

_____

8. Claire lives in a town where the streets are laid out on a grid and each block has the same length. One day she walked straight from her house for 7 blocks, then turned left and walked straight 6 blocks, then turned right and walked straight 4 blocks. Find the straight-line distance, in block lengths approximated to one decimal place, between Claire's house and her destination. Show your work.

_____

_____

_____

_____

9. The graph of the squaring function $y = x^2$ is shown.

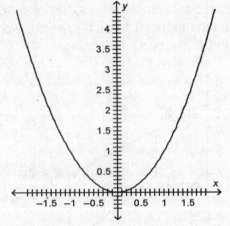

a. Describe how you can use the graph to show that the square roots of 4 are $\sqrt{4} = 2$ and $-\sqrt{4} = -2$.

_____

_____

b. Use the graph to estimate the square roots of 1.5 to the nearest tenth.

_____

_____

c. How does the graph show that 0 has only one square root?

_____

_____

10. After testing several numbers, Jacob wrote the following conjecture.

> A positive number n is equal to its square root if $n = 1$ and is greater than its square root otherwise.

a. Find the decimal approximation of $\sqrt{0.5}$ to the nearest tenth. Explain.

_____

_____

b. Does your answer to part a support Jacob's conjecture? Explain.

_____

_____

c. Consider the following proof.

$n > 1$	Start with a number greater than 1.
$n^2 > n$	Multiply both sides by n.
$\sqrt{n^2} > \sqrt{n}$	The greater number has the greater square root.
$n > \sqrt{n}$	The square root of a positive number squared is just the number.

This is a proof of what statement?

_____

_____

d. Write a proof of this statement:

> If a positive number is less than 1, then the number is less than its square root.

_____

_____

_____

_____

_____

_____

8.EE.1

SELECTED RESPONSE
Select the correct answer.

1. Use properties of exponents to write an equivalent expression for $11^2 \cdot 11^5$.

   Ⓐ 11^{10} Ⓒ 11^7

   Ⓑ $11^{\frac{2}{5}}$ Ⓓ 121^7

2. Use properties of exponents to write an equivalent expression for $5^4 \cdot 5^{-7}$.

   Ⓐ $\dfrac{1}{5^{28}}$ Ⓒ 5^{11}

   Ⓑ $\dfrac{1}{5^3}$ Ⓓ $5^{-\frac{4}{7}}$

3. Use properties of exponents to write an equivalent expression for $\dfrac{13^9}{13^6}$.

   Ⓐ $13^{\frac{3}{2}}$ Ⓒ 1^3

   Ⓑ 13^{15} Ⓓ 13^3

4. Use properties of exponents to write an equivalent expression for $(9^4)^6$.

   Ⓐ 9^{24} Ⓒ $\dfrac{1}{9^2}$

   Ⓑ 9^{10} Ⓓ $9^{\frac{2}{3}}$

5. Simplify the expression $(8^5)^0 + (7+3)^6 \cdot 10^{-8}$.

   Ⓐ $\dfrac{1}{100}$ Ⓒ 100

   Ⓑ $1\dfrac{1}{100}$ Ⓓ 101

Select all correct answers.

6. Which of the following expressions are equivalent to 14^6?

   Ⓐ $\dfrac{14^{18}}{14^3}$ Ⓓ $(14^4)^2$

   Ⓑ $\dfrac{(14^2)^5}{14^4}$ Ⓔ $(146)^0$

   Ⓒ $14^2 \cdot 14^3$ Ⓕ $14^{-5} \cdot 14^{11}$

7. Which of the following expressions have a value less than 1?

   Ⓐ $\dfrac{4^{11}}{4^{14}}$ Ⓓ $(2^3)^{-2}$

   Ⓑ $\dfrac{(3^5)^2}{3^4}$ Ⓔ $(5^4)^2 \cdot 5^{-11}$

   Ⓒ $4^{-1} \cdot 4^5$ Ⓕ $\dfrac{6^{-4} \cdot 6^6}{6^3}$

Select the correct answer for each lettered part.

8. Determine whether the properties of exponents are used correctly to simplify.

   a. $\dfrac{5^{10}}{5^5} = 5^2$ ○ Yes ○ No

   b. $\left(4^8\right)^3 = 4^{24}$ ○ Yes ○ No

   c. $10^{-4} = \dfrac{1}{4^{10}}$ ○ Yes ○ No

   d. $15^6 \cdot 15^3 = 15^{18}$ ○ Yes ○ No

   e. $\left(6^8\right)^0 = 1$ ○ Yes ○ No

CONSTRUCTED RESPONSE

9. Find the missing exponent. Explain.

   $$\dfrac{5^{11}}{5^?} = 5^4$$

   _____

   _____

10. Find the missing exponent. Explain your reasoning.

$$7^? \cdot (7^5)^4 = 7^{14}$$

_____

_____

11. Is $(17^3)^4 \cdot 17^{-4}$ equal to 17^8? Explain why or why not.

_____

_____

12. Is $\dfrac{3^{13}}{(3^5)^3}$ equal to 9? Explain why or why not.

_____

_____

13. Write three expressions that are equivalent to 2^6 using three different properties of integer exponents. Show why the expressions are equivalent.

_____

_____

14. Show whether the following expressions are equivalent to 3^4.

a. $\dfrac{3^2 \cdot 3^8}{(3^3)^2}$

_____

_____

b. $\left(\dfrac{3^9}{3^5 \cdot 3^6}\right)^2$

_____

_____

15. Three students simplified the expression $\dfrac{3^3}{9} \cdot 3^{-1}$ as shown below. Which student got the correct answer? What error(s) did each of the other students make, and what should they have done instead?

Student A:
$$\dfrac{3^3}{9} \cdot 3^{-1} = \dfrac{1^3}{3} \cdot 3^{-1} = \dfrac{1}{3} \cdot \dfrac{1}{3} = \dfrac{1}{9}$$

Student B: $\dfrac{3^3}{9} \cdot 3^{-1} = \dfrac{3^3 \cdot 3^{-1}}{9} = \dfrac{9^2}{9} = 9$

Student C:
$$\dfrac{3^3}{9} \cdot 3^{-1} = \dfrac{3^3}{3^2} \cdot 3^{-1} = 3^1 \cdot 3^{-1} = 3^0 = 1$$

_____

_____

_____

_____

16. The radius of the Sun is roughly 10^9 m, and the radius of Earth is roughly 10^7 m.

a. How many copies of Earth have to line up side-by-side in order to stretch across the face of the Sun? Explain your reasoning.

_____

_____

_____

b. How many copies of Earth could fit inside the Sun? Explain your reasoning.

_____

_____

_____

_____

8.EE.2

SELECTED RESPONSE
Select the correct answer.

1. Evaluate $\sqrt{\dfrac{1}{4}}$.

   (A) 2   (C) $\dfrac{1}{8}$

   (B) $\dfrac{1}{2}$ (D) $-\dfrac{1}{2}$

2. What is the value of x if $x^2 = 10$?

   (A) $\pm\sqrt{10}$ (C) 5

   (B) $\sqrt{10}$ (D) ± 5

3. Evaluate $\sqrt[3]{\dfrac{8}{27}}$.

   (A) $\dfrac{2}{9}$ (C) $\dfrac{3}{2}$

   (B) $\dfrac{2}{3}$ (D) 6

4. What is the value of x if $x^3 = 100$?

   (A) $\sqrt[3]{100}$ (C) 10

   (B) $\pm\sqrt[3]{100}$ (D) ± 10

5. Colin has a square garden with an area of 97 square feet. What is the length of each side of the garden?

   (A) 10 ft   (C) $\sqrt[3]{97}$ ft

   (B) $\sqrt{97}$ ft   (D) $-\sqrt{97}$ ft

Select all correct answers.

6. For which values of x is the expression $\sqrt{x}$ irrational?

   (A) 1

   (B) 2

   (C) 3

   (D) 4

   (E) 5

7. Which of the following expressions are equivalent to rational numbers?

   (A) $\sqrt[3]{0.008}$

   (B) $\sqrt{2}$

   (C) $\sqrt[3]{1}$

   (D) $\sqrt{3}$

   (E) $\sqrt[3]{9}$

   (F) $\sqrt{\dfrac{9}{64}}$

Match each radical expression with its rational equivalent.

_____ 8. $\sqrt{4}$ A $-\dfrac{1}{2}$

_____ 9. $\sqrt{81}$ B 0.05

_____ 10. $\sqrt{0.25}$ C 0.07

_____ 11. $\sqrt[3]{\dfrac{1}{64}}$ D $\dfrac{1}{4}$

    E 0.5

_____ 12. $\sqrt[3]{-\dfrac{1}{8}}$ F 0.7

    G 2

_____ 13. $\sqrt{0.49}$ H 9

CONSTRUCTED RESPONSE

14. Monica's rectangular living room is 12 ft by 15 ft. She has a square rug that covers $\dfrac{5}{9}$ of the area of the floor. What is the side length of the square rug? Show your work.

   _____

   _____

   _____

15. If $n^3 = 64$, what is the value of n^2? Explain.

   _____

   _____

16. Terry has two square sheets of wrapping paper. The area of the first is 36 in². The side length of the second is 1 inch longer than the first. Find the side length of each piece of wrapping paper and determine the area of the second piece.

_____

_____

_____

17. A rectangular prism measures 2 in. by 4 in. by 8 in. What is the side length of a cube with the same volume? Show your work.

_____

_____

_____

18. What values of x make the equation $x^2 = \sqrt[3]{125}$ a true statement? Show your work.

_____

_____

19. The numbers 1, 64, and 729 are both perfect squares and perfect cubes. Begin by finding the square roots and cube roots of 1, 64, and 729. Use the results to find a pattern. Then use the pattern to find the next number that is both a perfect square and a perfect cube. Show your work.

_____

_____

_____

20. Alex is accenting one wall of his room by painting a pattern of squares across the wall. He wants to alternate between red squares with an area of 25 square inches and blue squares with an area of 16 square inches.

   a. Find the side length of each square. Show your work.

   _____

   _____

   _____

   _____

   b. If he has enough room to place 12 of each type of square with no space between them, how long is the wall?

   _____

   _____

21. A fish tank is in the shape of a cube and has a volume of 27 ft³. It has glass on the bottom and the four vertical sides, but no top. Where two pieces of glass meet, the edge is reinforced with metal framing.

   a. What is the total area of glass needed to make the fish tank? Show your work.

   _____

   _____

   _____

   _____

   b. What is the total length of metal framing needed to reinforce the edges of the fish tank?

   _____

   _____

   _____

8.EE.3

SELECTED RESPONSE
Select the correct answer.

1. What is 12,325 written in scientific notation?
   - (A) 1.2325×10^{-4}
   - (C) 1.2325×10^4
   - (B) 12.325×10^3
   - (D) 1.2325×10^5

2. What is 0.005007 written in scientific notation?
   - (A) 5.007×10^3
   - (C) 5.007×10^{-4}
   - (B) 5.007×10^{-3}
   - (D) 500.7×10^{-5}

3. What is 1.0315×10^6 written in standard notation?
   - (A) 1,031,500
   - (C) 0.000010315
   - (B) 103,150
   - (D) 0.0000010315

4. What is 9.2568×10^{-3} written in standard notation?
   - (A) 0.0092568
   - (C) 0.92568
   - (B) 0.092568
   - (D) 9256.8

5. What is 8.305×10^{-7} written in standard notation?
   - (A) −83,050,000
   - (C) 0.00000008305
   - (B) 83,050,000
   - (D) 0.0000008305

Select all correct answers.

6. Which of the following statements are true?
   - (A) 3×10^4 is 50 times as great as 6×10^2.
   - (B) 5×10^2 is 100 times as great as 5×10^{-2}.
   - (C) 7×10^{-5} is 5000 times as great as 1.4×10^{-9}.
   - (D) 8×10^{-12} is 0.0001 times as great as 8×10^{-8}.
   - (E) 2×10^{-6} is 0.01 times as great as 2×10^{-4}.
   - (F) 1.8×10^{-3} is 0.00002 times as great as 9×10^4.

7. Which of the following measurements are equal to 0.000043 L?
   - (A) 4.3×10^2 L
   - (B) 4.3×10^{-4} L
   - (C) 4.3×10^{-5} L
   - (D) 4.3×10^{-2} mL
   - (E) 4.3×10^{-8} mL
   - (F) 4.3×10^{-10} mL

Match each number with its scientific notation equivalent.

____ 8. 3794

____ 9. 0.000003794

____ 10. 3,794,000

____ 11. 379,400

____ 12. 0.00000000003794

A 3.794×10^6
B 3.794×10^5
C 3.794×10^3
D 3.794×10^{-6}
E 3.794×10^{-10}
F 3.794×10^{-11}

CONSTRUCTED RESPONSE

13. A business sold for 32.6 million dollars. Write that number in scientific notation. Show your work.

_____

_____

14. Alea and Carlos are at the beach trying to guess the number of grains of sand. Alea estimates that there are 5×10^{15} grains of sand on the beach. Carlos estimates that there are 2×10^{12} grains of sand on the beach. How many times greater is Alea's estimate than Carlos's? Show your work.

_____

_____

15. Which is greater, 5.764×10^{-7} or 0.00000057652? Explain your reasoning.

16. Suppose a single bacterium occupies an area of 7.3×10^{-12} m². A colony of 100 of the same bacteria occupies an area of 7.3×10^{-6} square units. Which of the following is the best choice of units for the measurement 7.3×10^{-6}: square meters, square centimeters, or square millimeters? Explain your reasoning.

_____

_____

_____

17. Water samples were taken from a river that runs through a city and a town. The city has a population of 5.3×10^5, and the town has a population of 1.06×10^4. The water sample taken from the city had 6.28×10^6 bacteria per liter. The water sample taken from the town had 1.256×10^5 bacteria per liter.

a. How many times greater is the population of the city than the population of the town?

_____

b. How many times greater is the bacteria level in the city's water sample than the bacteria level in the town's water sample?

_____

c. Use these results to make a conjecture about the relationship between population and bacteria levels in the water.

_____

_____

_____

18. The mass of object A is 1.325×10^{-4} kg. The mass of object B is 3.3125×10^3 mg. Michael says that the mass of object B is 25,000,000 times greater than the mass of object A. Ana says that the mass of object B is 25 times greater than the mass of object A. Compare the masses of objects A and B to decide who is correct. Then find the error that the other person most likely made.

_____

_____

19. Mercury is 57,910,000 km from the Sun, Earth is 149,600,000 km from the Sun, and Saturn is 1,429,400,000 km from the Sun.

a. Write the distances in scientific notation.

_____

_____

b. Use the results from part a to find how many times greater Earth's distance from the Sun is than Mercury's distance from the Sun.

_____

c. Use the results from part a to find how many times greater Saturn's distance from the Sun is than Mercury's distance from the Sun.

_____

d. If you knew only the results of the comparisons in parts b and c and not the distances of the three planets from the Sun, what conclusion could you make about the relationship of Earth's distance from the Sun and Saturn's distance from the Sun? Explain.

_____

_____

8.EE.4

SELECTED RESPONSE
Select the correct answer.

1. Write the sum $3.75 \times 10^7 + 7.1 \times 10^6$ in scientific notation.

    (A) 44.6×10^6 (C) 1.085×10^8

    (B) 4.46×10^7 (D) 1.085×10^{14}

2. Write the difference $0.073 - 5.1 \times 10^{-3}$ in scientific notation.

    (A) -5.027×10^{-3} (C) 67.9×10^{-3}

    (B) 5.027×10^{-3} (D) 6.79×10^{-2}

3. Write the product $(8.4 \times 10^4)(9.5 \times 10^3)$ in scientific notation.

    (A) 79.8×10^7 (C) 79.8×10^{12}

    (B) 7.98×10^8 (D) 7.98×10^{13}

4. Write the quotient $\dfrac{6.25 \times 10^{-6}}{12.5}$ in scientific notation.

    (A) 5×10^{-7} (C) 2×10^{-6}

    (B) 0.5×10^{-6} (D) 2×10^6

5. When you use a calculator to find $(4.1 \times 10^{-3})(3.2 \times 10^{-6})$, what result does the calculator display?

    (A) 1.312E–8   (C) 1.312E10

    (B) 1.312E–6   (D) 1.312E12

Select all correct answers.

6. Identify all of the following values that are equivalent to $0.35 + 1.5 \times 10^{-3}$.

    (A) 1.85   (D) 3.515×10^{-1}

    (B) 0.3515   (E) 1.85E–3

    (C) 1.85×10^{-3} (F) 3.515E–1

7. Identify all of the following values that are equivalent to $\dfrac{0.75}{2.5 \times 10^6}$.

    (A) 3×10^{-7} (D) 30,000,000

    (B) 3×10^7 (E) 3E–7

    (C) 0.0000003   (F) 3E7

Match each number with its calculator notation equivalent.

____ 8. 9.8×10^4

____ 9. 0.000098

____ 10. 9.8×10^{-6}

____ 11. 9.8×10^7

____ 12. 980,000,000

   A 9.8E–6

   B 9.8E8

   C 9.8E4

   D 9.8E7

   E 9.8E9

   F 9.8E–5

CONSTRUCTED RESPONSE

13. An electronic component measures 1.2×10^{-5} m by 1.5×10^{-4} m. Find the area of this component in square millimeters, and express your answer using scientific notation. Show your work.

    _____

    _____

14. Simplify $\dfrac{3 \times 10^{-3} + 6 \times 10^{-2}}{(7 \times 10^4)(3 \times 10^8)}$. Show your work.

    _____

    _____

15. A company produces plastic discs for use in other products. The company produces 2×10^7 discs daily, each 1.55 mm thick.

    a. If the discs from one day's production were stacked one on top of the other, how tall would the stack be?

    _____

    b. Use the results from part a and the facts that 1 km = 1000 m and 1 m = 1000 mm to find the height of the stack in meters and kilometers.

    _____

    c. Which unit is most appropriate to use for the height of the stack? Explain.

    _____

    _____

16. Suppose a grain of dust is in the shape of a sphere with a radius 2×10^{-7} m. What is the volume of the dust grain? Use the volume formula $V = \frac{4}{3}\pi r^3$ with 3.14 as an approximation for π. Write your answer in scientific notation rounded to two decimal places.

_____

_____

17. Suppose a person drinks 8 glasses of water per day and each glass contains 3×10^2 mL of water.

a. How many milliliters of water does the person drink in 10 years? Use 365 days per year and express your answer using scientific notation.

_____

b. Of the units milliliters and liters, which is the more appropriate unit for this measurement? Explain your answer.

_____

_____

18. A computer store sells a flash drive that stores 2 gigabytes of data and another that stores 750 megabytes. Which flash drive should you purchase if you need to store a file that uses 9.65×10^7 bytes of storage space as well as 12 files that use 7.5×10^7 bytes each? Show your work. Use the facts that 1 gigabyte = 10^9 bytes and 1 megabyte = 10^6 bytes.

_____

_____

_____

19. On a recent math test, Alessandro was asked to simplify $\dfrac{7.2 \times 10^2 + 9.63 \times 10^3}{9 \times 10^9}$ and write his answer in standard form. Alessandro used a calculator and determined the answer to be 1.15E–6, which he wrote as 0.000000115. His answer was marked incorrect.

a. Simplify $\dfrac{7.2 \times 10^2 + 9.63 \times 10^3}{9 \times 10^9}$. Write your answer in standard form.

_____

_____

b. Compare your result from part a to Alessandro's answer and describe his likely error.

_____

_____

20. The Sun has a mass of 1.989×10^{30} kg and a diameter of 1,390,000 km. Earth has a mass of 5.972×10^{24} kg and a diameter of 12,756 km. Assuming the Sun and Earth are spheres, determine which has greater average density. Justify your answer. (Use the volume formula $V = \frac{4}{3}\pi r^3$ with 3.14 as an approximation for π. Also use the average density formula $D = \frac{m}{V}$, where m is the mass and V is the volume.)

_____

_____

_____

SELECTED RESPONSE
Select the correct answer.

1. The graph shows a proportional relationship. Use the graph to identify the unit rate.

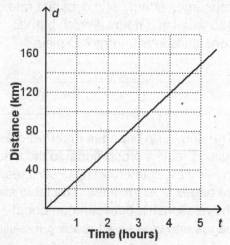

Ⓐ 30 hours per kilometer

Ⓑ 60 kilometers per hour

Ⓒ 30 kilometers per hour

Ⓓ $\frac{3}{2}$ kilometers per hour

2. The cost C, in dollars, of a prepaid cell phone call is proportional to the time t, in minutes, that the call lasts. The equation that represents this relationship for carrier A is $C_A = 0.15t$. The table shows the relationship for carrier B. Which carrier has a lower unit rate?

Time (minutes)	Cost (dollars)
2	0.24
5	0.60
10	1.20
30	3.60

Ⓐ Carrier A

Ⓑ Carrier B

Ⓒ Carrier A and carrier B have the same unit rate.

Ⓓ The relationship cannot be determined.

3. The number of pages p that a laser printer prints is proportional to the printing time t, in minutes. Printer A prints 104 pages in 4 minutes. The table shows the relationship between the amount of time and the number of pages printed for printer B. Which printer prints more slowly?

Time (minutes)	Pages printed
3	84
5	140
9	252
14	392

Ⓐ Printer A

Ⓑ Printer B

Ⓒ Printer A and printer B have the same unit rate.

Ⓓ The relationship cannot be determined.

Select all correct answers.

4. Which of the following proportional situations can be represented by this graph?

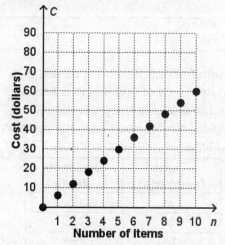

Ⓐ 2 pairs of headphones cost $12.

Ⓑ 24 carrots cost $4.

Ⓒ 3 packs of D batteries cost $18.

Ⓓ 6 bags of apples cost $36.

Ⓔ 6 jigsaw puzzles cost $10.

Name _____ Date _____ Class_____

CONSTRUCTED RESPONSE

5. The table shows the proportional relationship between an item's price p and the sales tax t charged for that item.

Price (dollars)	Sales Tax (dollars)
14	1.12
24	1.92
30	2.40
44	3.52

Graph the line that represents this relationship. What is the slope of the line? Interpret the slope.

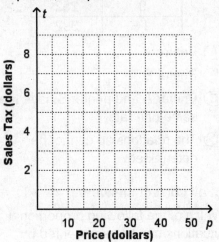

_____

_____

6. A remote-controlled truck travels at a constant rate of 108 feet in 6 seconds. The table shows the proportional relationship between distance traveled and time for a remote-controlled car.

Time (seconds)	Distance (feet)
3	63
5	105
8	168
12	252

Which travels faster, the car or truck? Explain.

_____

_____

7. Johan is comparing energy consumption for two different brands of refrigerators. The energy consumed e, in watts, is proportional to the time t, in hours, that the refrigerator is operating. The equation $e = 160t$ models the relationship for brand R. Another refrigerator, brand S, consumes energy at a constant rate of 435 watts in 3 hours. Which brand consumes less energy? Explain.

_____

_____

8. The number p of pages that Pedro and Allison read is proportional to the time t, in minutes, spent reading. Pedro reads 24 pages in 40 minutes. The table shows the relationship between number of pages and time spent reading for Allison.

Graph the lines that represent the relationships. Label each line with the name of the student it represents and the axes with the appropriate variables. Who reads faster? Explain.

Time (minutes)	Pages read
15	12
25	20
45	36
50	40

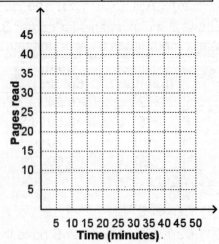

_____

_____

8.EE.6

SELECTED RESPONSE
Select the correct answer.

1. Why is the slope of the line shown the same between any two distinct points on the line?

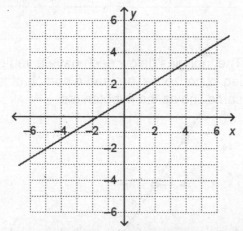

(A) All right triangles that have a vertical leg, a horizontal leg, and a portion of the line as the hypotenuse are similar, so the ratio of the length of the vertical leg to the length of the horizontal leg is always $\frac{5}{3}$.

(B) All right triangles that have a vertical leg, a horizontal leg, and a portion of the line as the hypotenuse are similar, so the ratio of the length of the vertical leg to the length of the horizontal leg is always $\frac{3}{5}$.

(C) All right triangles that have a vertical leg, a horizontal leg, and a portion of the line as the hypotenuse are congruent, so the ratio of the length of the vertical leg to the length of the horizontal leg is always $\frac{5}{3}$.

(D) All right triangles that have a vertical leg, a horizontal leg, and a portion of the line as the hypotenuse are congruent, so the ratio of the length of the vertical leg to the length of the horizontal leg is always $\frac{3}{5}$.

2. A line passes through the points (0, –4) and (2, –11). If (x, y) is an arbitrary point on the line other than (0, –4), which equation can you write for the line based on the fact that the slope of a line is constant?

(A) $\dfrac{y-0}{x-(-4)} = -\dfrac{7}{2}$

(B) $\dfrac{y-0}{x-(-4)} = -\dfrac{2}{7}$

(C) $\dfrac{y-(-4)}{x-0} = -\dfrac{7}{2}$

(D) $\dfrac{y-(-4)}{x-0} = -\dfrac{2}{7}$

3. A line that has a slope of $-\dfrac{5}{6}$ passes through the origin. Let (x, y) be an arbitrary point on the line other than the origin. Which of the following equations properly uses the fact that the slope of a line is constant to derive an equation of the line?

(A) $\dfrac{y}{x} = -\dfrac{5}{6}$

(B) $\dfrac{y}{x} = \dfrac{5}{6}$

(C) $\dfrac{y-5}{x+6} = 0$

(D) $\dfrac{x}{y} = -\dfrac{5}{6}$

4. For the line that passes through (0, 5) and has a slope of –3, you use the fact that the slope of a line is constant to derive the equation $\dfrac{y-5}{x-0} = -3$. What is an equivalent form of this equation?

(A) $y = 3x - 5$

(B) $y = 3x + 5$

(C) $y = -3x - 5$

(D) $y = -3x + 5$

Name _____   Date _____   Class _____

CONSTRUCTED RESPONSE

5. A line passes through the origin and the point (4, 8). Show how you can use this information, an arbitrary point (x, y) other than the origin, and the slope formula to find an equation of the line. Then rewrite the equation in the form $y = mx + b$.

_____

_____

6. Mi is deriving an equation of the line with a slope of $-\frac{1}{2}$ and a y-intercept of 4. She lets (x, y) be an arbitrary point on the line other than (0, 4) and proceeds as shown.

$$\frac{\text{change in } y}{\text{change in } x} = m$$

$$\frac{y - 0}{x - 4} = -\frac{1}{2}$$

$$\frac{y}{x - 4} \cdot (x - 4) = -\frac{1}{2} \cdot (x - 4)$$

$$y = -\frac{1}{2}x + 2$$

a. Looking at Mi's final equation, explain how you know she made a mistake.

_____

_____

b. Describe what Mi did wrong.

_____

_____

c. Derive a correct equation of the line.

_____

_____

7. A line that passes through the origin has slope m. Show how you can use this information, an arbitrary point (x, y) other than the origin, and the slope formula to derive an equation of the line. Then solve for y to rewrite the equation.

_____

_____

8. A line that passes through the point (0, b) has slope m. Show how you can use this information, an arbitrary point (x, y) other than (0, b), and the slope formula to derive an equation of the line. Then solve for y to rewrite the equation.

_____

_____

9. The triangles below each have a vertical leg, a horizontal leg, and a portion of the same line as the hypotenuse.

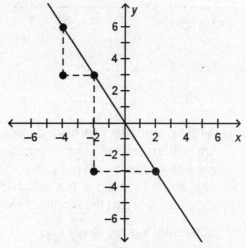

a. Explain how you know that the triangles are similar.

_____

_____

b. Use each triangle to determine the slope of the line. Explain why you would expect to get the same slope.

_____

_____

c. Use these results to generalize about the slope of a line calculated using any right triangle with a vertical leg, a horizontal leg, and a portion of the line as the hypotenuse.

_____

_____

_____

8.EE.7a

SELECTED RESPONSE
Select the correct answer.

1. How many solutions does the equation $5x + 17 = 4(3x - 1)$ have?

   (A) Infinitely many solutions

   (B) One solution

   (C) No solutions

   (D) The number of solutions cannot be determined.

2. How many solutions does the equation $7x - 11 = 5(x - 2) + 2x - 1$ have?

   (A) Infinitely many solutions

   (B) One solution

   (C) No solutions

   (D) The number of solutions cannot be determined.

3. Which of the following equations has exactly one solution?

   (A) $-7x + 2 = -3(x - 3) - 4x - 7$

   (B) $14x = 7(2x + 2)$

   (C) $5x + 3 = -2(2x + 3)$

   (D) $3(4x + 2) - 9 = 12x - 3$

4. What is a possible result of simplifying the equation $15x - 4 = 3(5x - 4)$?

   (A) $-4 = -4$

   (B) $x = 4$

   (C) $-4 = -12$

   (D) $x = 0$

5. Which of the following equations has no solutions?

   (A) $-6x + 1 = -3(2x + 1) + x$

   (B) $-5 + 14x = 7(2x) - 5$

   (C) $4x - 4 = -4(-x + 1)$

   (D) $-9x + 2 = -3(3x + 2)$

Select all correct answers.

6. Which of the following equations have no solutions?

   (A) $7x - 9 = 47$

   (B) $6x - 9 = 3(2x - 3)$

   (C) $-2x + 10 = 2(-x + 5) + 1$

   (D) $-x + 20 = x - 4$

   (E) $-5x - 5 = -5(x - 1)$

7. Suppose a linear equation in one variable, x, is simplified. Which of the following resulting equations would indicate that the original equation has infinitely many solutions?

   (A) $-4 = -4$

   (B) $11 = x$

   (C) $0 = 0$

   (D) $x = 0$

   (E) $1 = -1$

   (F) $x = x$

Select the correct answer for each lettered part.

8. Determine the number of solutions that each equation has.

   a. $7x + 5 = 2(4x + 3)$ ○ One solution ○ No solutions ○ Infinitely many solutions

   b. $x - 2(x - 6) = -x + 12$ ○ One solution ○ No solutions ○ Infinitely many solutions

   c. $8x + 5 = 5x - 7$ ○ One solution ○ No solutions ○ Infinitely many solutions

   d. $2(x - 1) = 3(x - 4)$ ○ One solution ○ No solutions ○ Infinitely many solutions

   e. $4x - 1 = 2(2x - 1)$ ○ One solution ○ No solutions ○ Infinitely many solutions

CONSTRUCTED RESPONSE

9. Write a linear equation in one variable that simplifies to the form $a = a$, where a is a number. Write your equation so that one side has parentheses and requires using the distributive property to simplify. How many solutions are there? Solve the equation and explain the result.

_____

_____

_____

10. Write a linear equation in one variable that has no solutions. Write your equation so that one side of the equation has both a variable term with a coefficient other than 1 and a constant term. Show your work. Explain why there are no solutions.

_____

_____

_____

11. Write a linear equation in one variable that has one solution. Write your equation so that there is a variable term and a constant term on each side of the equation. Solve your equation.

_____

_____

12. Sarah attempted to solve the equation $-x + 5(x + 6) = 4x + 30$ as shown, and concluded that there are no solutions.

$$-x + 5(x + 6) = 4x + 30$$
$$-x + 5x + 6 = 4x + 30$$
$$4x - 4x + 6 = 4x - 4x + 30$$
$$6 = 30$$

Solve the equation, identify Sarah's error, and find the correct number of solutions.

_____

13. Mark and Zoe are hiking a trail. Mark starts before Zoe. The expression $2t + 100$ represents how far, in meters, Mark has hiked t seconds after Zoe starts, and $2t$ represents how far Zoe has hiked t seconds after starting. Is there a time during the hike when Mark and Zoe have hiked the same distance? Explain.

_____

_____

14. a. How many solutions are there to $8x - 7 = 2(2x + 7) - 5$? Show your work, and explain your reasoning.

_____

_____

   b. Change one number in the equation in part a so the number of solutions for the resulting equation is different than in part a. How many solutions does your equation have? Show your work, and explain your reasoning.

_____

_____

   c. Change one number in your equation in part b so the number of solutions for the new equation differs from the equations in parts a and b. How many solutions does this equation have? Show your work, and explain your reasoning.

_____

_____

15. What are the conditions for the equation $ax + b = c(x + d)$, where a, b, c, and d are numbers and x is a variable, to have no solutions? One solution? Infinitely many solutions? Explain by simplifying the equation for each set of conditions.

_____

SELECTED RESPONSE
Select the correct answer.

1. What are the steps to solving the equation $\frac{3}{8}x + \frac{15}{2} = 18$?

   Ⓐ Subtract $\frac{15}{2}$ from both sides of the equation, and then multiply both sides of the equation by $-\frac{3}{8}$.

   Ⓑ Add $\frac{15}{2}$ to both sides of the equation, and then multiply both sides of the equation by $\frac{3}{8}$.

   Ⓒ Subtract $\frac{15}{2}$ from both sides of the equation, and then multiply both sides of the equation by $\frac{8}{3}$.

   Ⓓ Add $\frac{15}{2}$ to both sides of the equation, and then multiply both sides of the equation by $\frac{8}{3}$.

2. How do the solutions of the equations $\frac{1}{3}(x-9) = 2x+7$ and $\frac{4}{3}(x+4) = -4x$ compare?

   Ⓐ The solution of the equation $\frac{1}{3}(x-9) = 2x+7$ is greater than the solution of $\frac{4}{3}(x+4) = -4x$.

   Ⓑ The solution of the equation $\frac{1}{3}(x-9) = 2x+7$ is less than the solution of $\frac{4}{3}(x+4) = -4x$.

   Ⓒ The solutions are equal.

   Ⓓ The relationship cannot be determined.

3. A rectangle has length $\frac{1}{2}x + 5$ and width $\frac{1}{4}x + 4$. If the perimeter of the rectangle is 42 meters, what are the length and the width of the rectangle?

   Ⓐ Length: 8 meters; width: 13 meters
   Ⓑ Length: 13 meters; width: 8 meters
   Ⓒ Length: 15 meters; width: 27 meters
   Ⓓ Length: 27 meters; width: 15 meters

Select all correct answers.

4. Which of the following equations have a positive solution?

   Ⓐ $\frac{1}{2}x + 5 = \frac{1}{2}(2-x)$

   Ⓑ $\frac{2}{5}(x+5) = \frac{1}{5}(x+4)$

   Ⓒ $\frac{3}{2}(x-8) = \frac{1}{4}x + 3$

   Ⓓ $\frac{1}{3}x + 6 = \frac{3}{4}(x+8)$

   Ⓔ $\frac{5}{2}(x-3) = \frac{5}{3}x - \frac{5}{2}$

CONSTRUCTED RESPONSE

5. Solve the equation $-\frac{3}{5}(x-10) = \frac{6}{5}x + 2$. Show your work.

   _____

   _____

   _____

6. Do the equations $\frac{2}{3}(x-6)+3 = 4x-4$ and $\frac{2}{3}x - 6 + 3 = 4x - 4$ have the same solution? Explain by comparing the two equations.

   _____

   _____

7. The area A of a trapezoid is given by $A = \frac{1}{2}h(b_1 + b_2)$, where h is the height and b_1 and b_2 are the lengths of the bases. What is the length of the other base if the area is 98 square meters, the height is 7 meters, and the length of one base is 11 meters? Show your work.

_____

_____

_____

8. Ryan and Nate are swimming in a lake. Ryan swims $\frac{5}{4}$ meters per second. Nate swims $\frac{4}{5}$ meter per second. If Nate starts 45 meters ahead of Ryan, how long does it take Ryan to catch Nate? How far must Ryan swim to catch him? Explain.

_____

_____

9. a. Use the distributive property to solve $\frac{1}{4}(x - 7) + 5 = \frac{7}{8}x$. Show your work.

_____

_____

b. Solve the equation from part a by first multiplying both sides by the least common denominator of $\frac{1}{4}$ and $\frac{7}{8}$. Show your work, and compare your result here with that from part a.

_____

_____

c. What property of equality justifies the first step that you took in part b? How is this step helpful?

_____

_____

10. Christian claims he found the solution of the equation $\frac{3}{4}x + 5 = \frac{1}{2}(x - 8)$. His work is shown below. Identify his error, correct the error, and find the actual solution. Show your work.

$$\frac{3}{4}x + 5 = \frac{1}{2}(x - 8)$$
$$\frac{3}{4}x + 5 = \frac{1}{2}x - 4$$
$$\frac{3}{4}x + \frac{1}{2}x + 5 = \frac{1}{2}x + \frac{1}{2}x - 4$$
$$\frac{5}{4}x + 5 - 5 = -4 - 5$$
$$\frac{5}{4}x = -9$$
$$x = -\frac{36}{5}$$

_____

_____

11. The booster club sets up a hot dog stand for fundraising at a middle school. The club receives $12 in donations while members set up the stand. The club sells hot dogs for $1.75. Each hot dog costs the club $0.50, and other supplies cost $57. The club wants to know how many hot dogs they must sell to break even.

a. Write an equation that represents this situation, where h represents the number of hot dogs sold.

_____

b. Find the number of hot dogs the booster club must sell to break even.

_____

c. If the booster club wants to break even by only selling half the number of hot dogs from part b, how much should it charge for each hot dog? Use p to represent the new price for each hot dog. Show your work.

_____

_____

8.EE.8a

SELECTED RESPONSE

Select the correct answer.

1. How can you tell if an ordered pair is a solution of a system of linear equations by examining the graphs of the equations?

   (A) Neither line passes through the point represented by the ordered pair.

   (B) Just one of the lines passes through the point represented by the ordered pair.

   (C) Both lines pass through the point represented by the ordered pair.

   (D) You cannot tell whether an ordered pair is a solution of a system of linear equations by examining the graphs of the equations.

2. Does the ordered pair $(-5, 3)$ satisfy the system of equations? Explain.

$$\begin{cases} y = -2x - 1 \\ y = -\dfrac{3}{5}x \end{cases}$$

   (A) Yes, because the ordered pair $(-5, 3)$ satisfies both equations of the system.

   (B) No, because the ordered pair $(-5, 3)$ satisfies only the equation $y = -2x - 1$.

   (C) No, because the ordered pair $(-5, 3)$ satisfies only the equation $y = -\dfrac{3}{5}x$.

   (D) No, because the ordered pair $(-5, 3)$ satisfies neither equation of the system.

3. Which ordered pair is the solution of the system of linear equations?

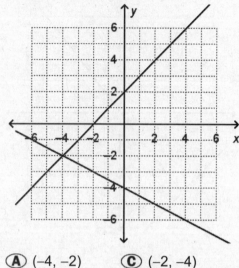

   (A) $(-4, -2)$ (C) $(-2, -4)$

   (B) $(-4, 2)$ (D) $(2, 4)$

Select all correct answers.

4. For which of the following systems of equations is the ordered pair $(-8, 4)$ a solution?

   (A) $\begin{cases} 3x + 4y = 8 \\ -3x + 4y = -40 \end{cases}$

   (B) $\begin{cases} -2x - 3y = 4 \\ 7x + 4y = -40 \end{cases}$

   (C) $\begin{cases} -5x + 2y = 32 \\ 6x - 7y = -20 \end{cases}$

   (D) $\begin{cases} -3x + 5y = 44 \\ 6x - 5y = -68 \end{cases}$

   (E) $\begin{cases} 3x + 8y = 56 \\ -x + 9y = 28 \end{cases}$

CONSTRUCTED RESPONSE

5. Suppose that a graph of a system of linear equations consists of two lines that coincide. How many solutions does the system have? Explain your reasoning.

_____

_____

6. Is the ordered pair (−5, −4) a solution of the system of linear equations whose graph is shown? Explain your reasoning.

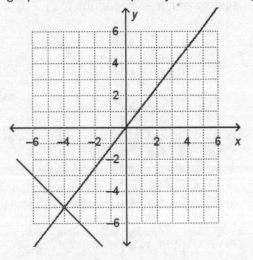

_____

_____

7. Matt concluded that the system whose graph is shown has no solution. Is he correct? Explain your reasoning.

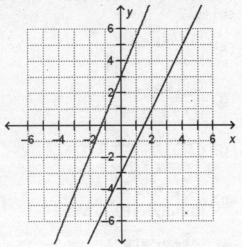

_____

_____

8. Can the same system of linear equations have the ordered pairs (3, 7) and (6, 13) as solutions? Explain your reasoning by providing an example.

_____

_____

9. The solution of a system of linear equations is (−4, 2).

   a. Draw two lines that could represent this system of equations.

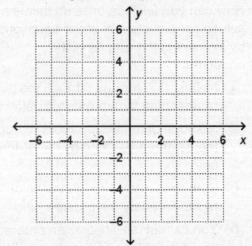

   b. Explain why your graph is correct.

_____

_____

10. Chandler says the solution of the system of equations $y = -x - 3$ and $y = 3x + 1$ is (−2, −1) because the graphs of the equations intersect at the point (−2, −1).

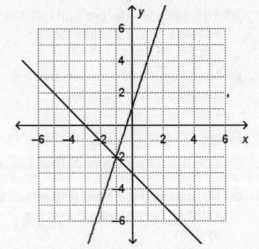

   a. Identify and correct Chandler's error.

_____

   b. Explain how one of the lines could be translated to make Chandler's solution of the system correct.

_____

8.EE.8b

SELECTED RESPONSE
Select the correct answer.

1. What solution(s) does the system of equations have?

$$\begin{cases} -2x+5y=10 \\ -4x+10y=20 \end{cases}$$

Ⓐ There are infinitely many solutions.

Ⓑ The only solution is (5, 4).

Ⓒ The only solution is (10, 6).

Ⓓ There are no solutions.

2. To solve the system of equations

$$\begin{cases} 4x+y=-12 \\ 5x+2y=25 \end{cases}$$, what expression should

be substituted for y in the equation $5x + 2y = 25$?

Ⓐ $-\dfrac{y}{4}-3$　　　Ⓒ $-\dfrac{5}{2}x+\dfrac{25}{2}$

Ⓑ $-4x - 12$　　　Ⓓ $-\dfrac{2}{5}y+5$

3. Trudy and Xander are saving money from their newspaper route earnings. Their savings s, in dollars, are related to the time t, in weeks, after they start working. Trudy's savings are given by the equation $s = 40t + 50$, and Xander's savings are given by the equation $s = 35t + 100$. What is the meaning of the solution of the system of equations?

Ⓐ Trudy and Xander both have $450 saved after 10 weeks of working on their newspaper routes.

Ⓑ Trudy and Xander both have $10 saved after 450 weeks of working on their newspaper routes.

Ⓒ Trudy and Xander both have $170 saved after 2 weeks of working on their newspaper routes.

Ⓓ Trudy and Xander both have $130 saved after 2 weeks of working on their newspaper routes.

Select the correct answer for each lettered part.

4. Determine the number of solutions of each system of equations.

a. $\begin{cases} -14x-20y=42 \\ -14x-20y=42 \end{cases}$　　○ Infinitely many solutions　　○ One solution　　○ No solutions

b. $\begin{cases} x+y=5 \\ -2x-2y=10 \end{cases}$　　○ Infinitely many solutions　　○ One solution　　○ No solutions

c. $\begin{cases} x+y=6 \\ x+2y=6 \end{cases}$　　○ Infinitely many solutions　　○ One solution　　○ No solutions

d. $\begin{cases} -x-y=-14 \\ -x-y=14 \end{cases}$　　○ Infinitely many solutions　　○ One solution　　○ No solutions

e. $\begin{cases} 3x+y=13 \\ 6x+2y=26 \end{cases}$　　○ Infinitely many solutions　　○ One solution　　○ No solutions

Name _____ Date _____ Class _____

CONSTRUCTED RESPONSE

5. Estimate the solution of the system of equations by examining its graph. Round each coordinate to the nearest 0.5.

$$\begin{cases} y = 2x + 4 \\ y = \dfrac{1}{3}x - 2 \end{cases}$$

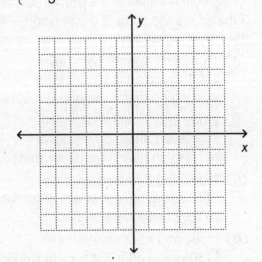

_____

6. Solve the system algebraically.

$$\begin{cases} -x + y = 4 \\ 5x + 2y = 1 \end{cases}$$

_____
_____
_____
_____
_____
_____

7. Solve the system of equations by inspection. Explain your reasoning.

$$\begin{cases} -2x + 4y = 5 \\ -2x + 4y = 6 \end{cases}$$

_____
_____

8. The cost c, in dollars, of a taxi ride is related to the distance d, in miles, of the ride. The cost for taxi A is given by the equation $c = 3.5d + 2$, and the cost for taxi B is given by $c = 3d + 5$. For what distance is the cost of each taxi ride the same? How much would this trip cost?

_____
_____

9. Dylan says that $(-1, 7)$ is the solution of the system of equations $\begin{cases} 2x - 3y = -24 \\ x + 4y = 27 \end{cases}$ when each coordinate of the solution is estimated to the nearest 0.5. Graph the system of linear equations. Is Dylan's estimate correct? Explain.

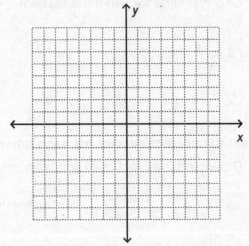

10. Two boats leave a marina 2 hours apart. The distance d, in miles, of each boat from the marina at time t, measured in hours since the second boat left the marina, is given by $d = 8(t + 2)$ for the first boat and $d = 12t$ for the second.

   a. Find the solution of the system of equations algebraically.

   _____

   b. What is the meaning of the solution?

   _____
   _____
   _____

8.EE.8c

SELECTED RESPONSE

Select the correct answer.

1. Which pair of points forms a line that does not intersect the line that passes through the points (5, 7) and (7, 7)?

    Ⓐ (−4, −5) and (−1, −2)

    Ⓑ (−5, 3) and (−5, 8)

    Ⓒ (−2, −9) and (3, −4)

    Ⓓ (8, −9) and (11, −9)

2. Skylar is buying watermelon and pineapple for a fruit salad. Watermelon costs $0.59 per pound, and pineapple costs $2.29 per pound. Skylar buys 7 pounds of fruit and spends $9.23. How much does Skylar spend just on pineapple?

    Ⓐ $2.36   Ⓒ $4.00

    Ⓑ $3.00   Ⓓ $6.87

3. The line that passes through the points (−5, −6) and (−3, 2) and the line with equation $y = x − 4$ intersect at what point?

    Ⓐ (−5, −6)   Ⓒ (−3, 2)

    Ⓑ (2, −2)   Ⓓ (−6, −10)

4. There are 25 coins inside a container. Some of the coins are nickels, and the rest are quarters. The value of the coins is $4.05. Let n represent the number of nickels, and let q represent the number of quarters. Which system of equations represents this situation?

    Ⓐ $\begin{cases} n - q = 25 \\ 0.05n + 0.25q = 4.05 \end{cases}$

    Ⓑ $\begin{cases} n + q = 4.05 \\ 0.05n + 0.25q = 25 \end{cases}$

    Ⓒ $\begin{cases} n + q = 25 \\ 0.05n + 0.25q = 4.05 \end{cases}$

    Ⓓ $\begin{cases} n + q = 25 \\ 5n + 25q = 4.05 \end{cases}$

Use the following information to match each statement with the corresponding system of equations.

While on vacation, Rosa stopped at a souvenir shop to buy keychains and refrigerator magnets for family members and friends. Keychains cost $2 each, and refrigerator magnets cost $1 each. Let x represent the number of keychains that Rosa bought, and let y represent the number of refrigerator magnets.

_____ 5. Rosa bought 12 items and paid a total of $18.

_____ 6. Rosa bought 12 more refrigerator magnets than keychains and paid a total of $18.

_____ 7. Rosa bought 12 items and paid $18 more for the keychains than for the refrigerator magnets.

_____ 8. Rosa bought 18 items and paid $12 more for the refrigerator magnets than for the keychains.

A $\begin{cases} x + y = 12 \\ -2x + y = 18 \end{cases}$

B $\begin{cases} x + y = 12 \\ 2x - y = 18 \end{cases}$

C $\begin{cases} x + y = 12 \\ 2x + y = 18 \end{cases}$

D $\begin{cases} x + y = 18 \\ 2x + y = 12 \end{cases}$

E $\begin{cases} -x + y = 12 \\ 2x + y = 18 \end{cases}$

F $\begin{cases} x + y = 18 \\ -2x + y = 12 \end{cases}$

CONSTRUCTED RESPONSE

9. Does the line that passes through the points (0, 12) and (7, 10) intersect the line $2x + 7y = 21$? Explain your reasoning.

_____

_____

10. Jesse owns a sporting goods store that sells skis and snowboards. The store earns a profit of $52 for each pair of skis sold and a profit of $64 for each snowboard sold. If Jesse's store sells a total of 83 pairs of skis and snowboards and earns a profit of $4892 in November, how many pairs of skis and how many snowboards did the store sell that month?

_____

_____

11. Dan is moving old monitors and printers from an office to the local electronics recycling center. Dan has to move a total number of 60 printers and monitors with a combined weight of 1750 pounds. One monitor weighs 35 pounds, and a printer weighs 25 pounds. Does Dan recycle a greater weight of printers or monitors? Explain using a system of equations.

_____

_____

12. Two containers are being filled with water. One begins with 8 gallons of water and is filled at a rate of 3.5 gallons per minute. The other begins with 24 gallons and is filled at 3.25 gallons per minute.

   a. Write an equation that represents the amount of water w, in gallons, with respect to time t, in minutes, for each container.

   b. Solve the system of equations algebraically. Show your work.

_____

_____

_____

_____

   c. How long would it take for both of the containers to have the same amount of water? How much water would be in each container?

_____

13. Marie, a police officer, spots a speeding car and starts chasing it. The speeding car travels at a constant speed of 130 feet per second. Marie's car reaches a constant speed of 145 feet per second 1725 feet from the start of the chase. During that time, the speeding car has traveled 3150 feet.

   a. Write an equation for each car that relates the distance d, in feet, from where the chase starts to the time t, in seconds, after Marie's car reaches a speed of 145 feet per second.

_____

   b. Solve the system of equations algebraically. Show your work.

_____

_____

_____

_____

   c. What is the meaning of the solution from part b?

_____

_____

8.F.1

SELECTED RESPONSE
Select the correct answer.

1. Use the graph to explain why y is or is not a function of x.

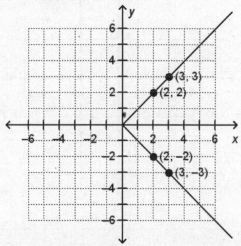

(A) y is a function of x because both (2, 2) and (2, −2) have the same x-coordinate.

(B) y is a function of x because for each y-coordinate, there is exactly one x-coordinate.

(C) y is not a function of x because both (2, 2) and (2, −2) have the same x-coordinate.

(D) y is not a function of x because for each x-coordinate, there is exactly one y-coordinate.

2. What is a function?

(A) A function assigns to each input exactly one output.

(B) A function assigns to each input at least one output.

(C) A function assigns outputs to inputs.

(D) A function assigns to each input more than one output.

3. Explain whether the table represents a function.

Input	Output
−2	4
−1	2
0	0
1	−2
2	−4

(A) The table represents a function because each input has exactly one output assigned to it.

(B) The table represents a function because the inputs and outputs are integers.

(C) The table does not represent a function because there are positive inputs that have negative outputs and there are negative inputs that have positive outputs.

(D) The table does not represent a function because there are inputs that have more than one output assigned to them.

Select all correct answers.

4. Which of the following sets of ordered pairs (x, y) represent y as a function of x?

(A) {(1, 2), (1, 3), (1, 4), (1, 5)}

(B) {(2.5, 8), (3.5, 8), (2.5, 2), (4.5, 2)}

(C) {(−1, 1), (0, 0), (1, 1), (2, 2)}

(D) {(−5, −7.0), (−4, −5.6), (−3, −4.2), (−2, −2.8)}

(E) {(4, −2), (1, −1), (0, 0), (4, 2)}

(F) $\left\{ \left(\frac{1}{2}, 0 \right), \left(1, \frac{1}{2} \right), \left(\frac{3}{2}, 1 \right), \left(2, \frac{3}{2} \right) \right\}$

Name _____ Date _____ Class _____

CONSTRUCTED RESPONSE

5. Can a function assign multiple inputs to the same output? Explain.

_____

_____

_____

6. Yen says the following set of ordered pairs does not represent a function because the ordered pairs (1, 2) and (3, 2) have different *x*-values but the same *y*-value.

{(0, 0), (0, 1), (1, 2), (3, 2)}

a. Is Yen correct about the set not representing a function?

_____

b. Is Yen's reasoning correct? If not, explain why and correct her reasoning.

_____

_____

7. Add a line to the mapping diagram so that it no longer represents a function. Explain why it no longer represents a function.

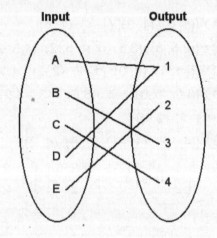

_____

_____

8. A horizontal line and a vertical line are shown. Which line represents a function and which does not? Explain your reasoning.

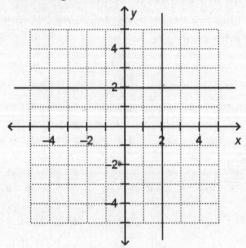

_____

_____

_____

9. A scientist studying snakes records two sets of data as described below. Tell whether each set of data necessarily represents a function. Explain your reasoning.

a. The scientist records the age *a*, in months, and the length ℓ, in inches, of a single snake over the course of its life. The scientist reports the data in the form (a, ℓ).

_____

_____

b. The scientist records, all on the same day, the age *a*, in months, and the length ℓ, in inches, of each snake in a collection of snakes. The scientist reports the data in the form (a, ℓ).

_____

_____

_____

SELECTED RESPONSE
Select the correct answer.

1. Which function's graph has the same *x*-intercept as the line shown?

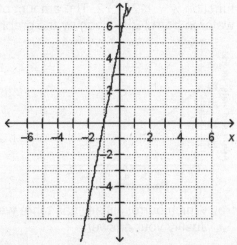

Ⓐ $y = -5x - 5$ Ⓒ $y = 5x - 1$

Ⓑ $y = -5x + 5$ Ⓓ $y = \frac{1}{5}x + 5$

2. The rate of change for linear function A is $\frac{1}{3}$. Its graph has a *y*-intercept of 1. The graph below represents function B. What do the graphs of these two functions have in common?

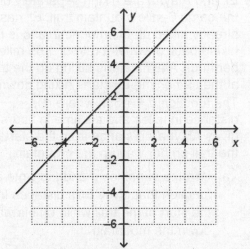

Ⓐ The point (1, 4)
Ⓑ The *y*-intercept
Ⓒ The slope
Ⓓ The *x*-intercept

3. The graph of a linear function passes through the points whose coordinates are given in the table. The graph of which function has the same slope as the graph of the function represented by the table?

x	0	1	2	3
y	−0.5	−0.25	0	0.25

Ⓐ $y = -0.25x - 2$ Ⓒ $y = 4x - 5$

Ⓑ $y = 0.25x + 5$ Ⓓ $y = -4x + 3$

4. The rate of change for linear function A is −6. Its graph crosses the *y*-axis at (0, 12). Linear function B is represented by the table shown. What do the graphs of functions A and B have in common?

x	0	2	4	6
y	3	9	15	21

Ⓐ The *y*-intercept
Ⓑ The point (1, 6)
Ⓒ The *x*-intercept
Ⓓ The slope

Select all correct answers.

5. Which functions have graphs that share the *x*-intercept, *y*-intercept, or slope with the graph of the function shown?

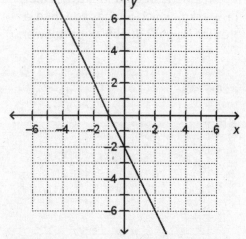

Ⓐ $y = 2x - 2$ Ⓓ $y = -2x + 2$

Ⓑ $y = -\frac{1}{2}x + 2$ Ⓔ $y = \frac{1}{2}x + 2$

Ⓒ $y = 2x + 2$ Ⓕ $y = \frac{1}{2}x - 2$

CONSTRUCTED RESPONSE

6. Martha and Howard are running at a constant speed in a marathon. Martha runs at 4.5 miles per hour. Howard's progress is shown in the table.

Time (hours)	Distance (miles)
1	5
2	10
3	15

   a. Who runs faster? Explain.

   _____

   b. If Martha and Howard are 5 hours into the marathon, how far has each run?

   _____

7. Ivy is growing up two sides of a house. Side A is sunny, and side B is shady. The ivy on side A grows up from the ground at a rate of 2 inches per week. At the time that the ivy on side A starts growing, the ivy on side B has already been growing. The graph shows the height h, in inches above the ground, of the ivy growing on side B at time t, in weeks. (Note that on this graph, $t = 0$ is the time at which the ivy on side A begins to grow.) After 11 weeks, which ivy has reached a greater height? Justify your answer.

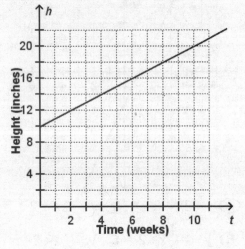

   _____

   _____

8. Rain barrels A and B are filled with water. A different pump removes water from each barrel at a different constant rate. The amount of water w, in liters, in barrel A at time t, in minutes, is given by the function $w = -12t + 72$. The amount of water in barrel B is given by the graph.

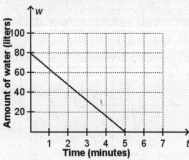

   a. Which barrel initially has more water? Justify your answer.

   _____

   b. Which barrel is emptied at the greater rate? Justify your answer.

   _____

   c. Which barrel will be empty first? Justify your answer.

   _____

   _____

9. Eli and Alayna are hiking separately on the same 6-mile mountain trail. Eli has already hiked up the mountain and is now hiking back down at a rate of 1.65 miles per hour. Alayna starts hiking up the trail at the same time Eli starts hiking down. The function $d = 1.35t$, where d is distance in miles and t is time in hours, gives Alayna's distance from the start of the trail on her way up the mountain.

   a. Use the variables d and t to write a function that gives Eli's distance from the start of the trail while on his way down the mountain.

   _____

   b. At what point on the trail do Eli and Alayna meet? Explain.

   _____

8.F.3

SELECTED RESPONSE
Select the correct answer.

1. Which equation does not represent a linear function?

   Ⓐ $y = 2$ Ⓒ $y = x$

   Ⓑ $y = x^2 + 9$ Ⓓ $y = -8x + 1$

2. In the right triangle shown, the equation for the hypotenuse is $y = \dfrac{4}{5}x + 1$, the equation for the longer leg is $y = -3$, and the equation for the shorter leg is $x = 5$. Which of these equations, if any, does not represent a linear function?

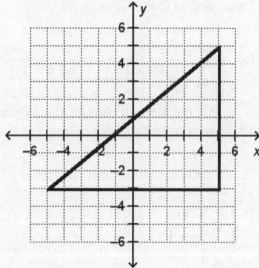

   Ⓐ The equation for the hypotenuse does not represent a linear function.

   Ⓑ The equation for the longer leg does not represent a linear function.

   Ⓒ The equation for the shorter leg does not represent a linear function.

   Ⓓ Each of the equations represents a linear function.

3. Which points are on the graph of a linear function?

   Ⓐ (−2, 11), (−1, 9), and (0, 7)

   Ⓑ (−1, 2), (0, 3), and (1, 2)

   Ⓒ (1, 1), (1, 3), and (1, 6)

   Ⓓ (−5, 3), (−3, 0), and (−1, −6)

Select all correct answers.

4. Which equations represent a function that is not linear?

   Ⓐ $y = 3x + 12$

   Ⓑ $y = -6x + x^2$

   Ⓒ $y = x^2 + 2$

   Ⓓ $y = 10x$

   Ⓔ $y = x^3$

   Ⓕ $y = 9$

Select the correct answer for each lettered part.

5. Indicate whether each equation represents a linear function.

   a. $y = 5x$ ○ Yes   ○ No

   b. $y = 2x^2 - 6$ ○ Yes   ○ No

   c. $y = -3x + 12$ ○ Yes   ○ No

   d. $x + 7y = 21$ ○ Yes   ○ No

   e. $xy = 13$ ○ Yes   ○ No

   f. $x = -3$ ○ Yes   ○ No

CONSTRUCTED RESPONSE

6. Do the ordered pairs in the table of values represent a linear function? Explain.

x	1	2	3	4	5	6
y	3	6	11	18	27	38

_____

_____

_____

7. Oliver says that the equations $y = 1$ and $x = 1$ both represent linear functions. Is Oliver correct? Explain.

_____

_____

_____

Name _____ Date _____ Class _____

8. Do the three points shown lie on the graph of a linear function? If so, find an equation of the function. If not, explain why not.

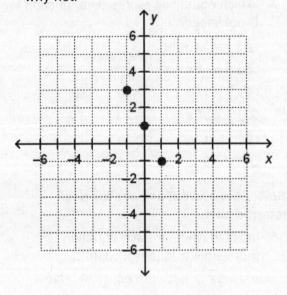

_____

_____

_____

9. a. Write $6x - 2y = 0$ in slope-intercept form, if possible.

_____

b. Write $x = 11y - 2$ in slope-intercept form, if possible.

_____

c. Write $4xy = 10$ in slope-intercept form, if possible.

_____

d. Write $x + 2 = 0$ in slope-intercept form, if possible.

_____

e. Which equations represent linear functions? Explain.

_____

_____

10. Vladimir and Cheryl are walking down the street. Vladimir walks at a speed of 4 miles per hour, and Cheryl walks at a speed of 3 miles per hour.

a. Write an equation for the distance d, in miles, each person walks over time t, in hours.

_____

b. Do the equations represent linear functions? Explain.

_____

11. An object is dropped from a height of 64 feet. As it falls, the function $h = 64 - 16t^2$ models the object's height h, in feet, at time t, in seconds.

a. Use the function to complete the table of values.

t	0	0.5	1	1.5	2
h					

b. Plot the ordered pairs in the table on the coordinate plane.

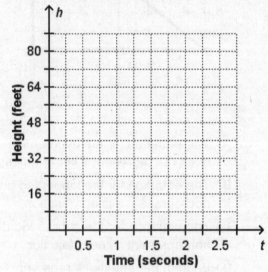

c. Does the equation represent a linear function? Use slope to explain why or why not.

_____

_____

8.F.4

SELECTED RESPONSE
Select the correct answer.

1. Vincent's savings over several weeks are shown in the table. If a linear function models Vincent's savings over time, how much money did he initially have?

Time (weeks)	2	4	6	8	10
Savings (dollars)	75	115	155	195	235

Ⓐ $0   ⓒ $35

Ⓑ $20   Ⓓ $75

2. Lynn is walking from her house to the grocery store. The table shows the distance she has left to walk. What is the rate of change for the linear function represented by the table?

Time (minutes)	Distance (blocks)
2	9
4	8
6	7
8	6

Ⓐ −2 blocks per minute

Ⓑ −0.5 block per minute

ⓒ 0.5 block per minute

Ⓓ 2 blocks per minute

3. The graph shows a burning candle's height h, in centimeters, at time t, in hours. What linear function does the graph represent?

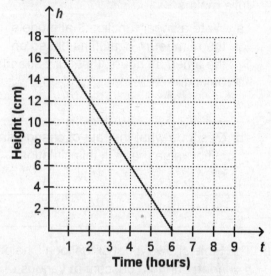

Ⓐ $h = -3t + 18$ ⓒ $h = -3t + 6$

Ⓑ $h = 3t + 18$ Ⓓ $h = 3t + 6$

4. The table shows the average number s of sandwiches a deli sells over time t, in minutes. What linear function does the table represent?

Time (minutes)	3	6	9	12
Sandwiches sold	19	25	31	37

Ⓐ $s = -2t + 13$ ⓒ $s = 2t$

Ⓑ $s = 13t + 2$ Ⓓ $s = 2t + 13$

Sue likes to hike and scuba dive. Match each description of Sue's activity with the function modeling Sue's elevation E, in feet, at time t, in minutes.

_____ 5. While hiking on a hill, Sue starts at an elevation of 100 feet and ascends at a rate of 20 feet per minute.

_____ 6. While scuba diving, Sue starts at an elevation of 100 feet below sea level and ascends at a rate of 20 feet per minute.

_____ 7. While hiking on a hill, Sue starts at an elevation of 100 feet and descends at a rate of 20 feet per minute.

_____ 8. While scuba diving, Sue starts at sea level and descends at a rate of 20 feet per minute.

A $E = 20t$

B $E = 20t + 100$

C $E = 20t - 100$

D $E = -20t$

E $E = -20t + 100$

F $E = -20t - 100$

CONSTRUCTED RESPONSE

9. Julie is making muffins for a bake sale. It takes her 30 minutes to make a dozen muffins. Tim had already made 36 muffins, which he adds to the amount Julie makes.

a. Write a linear function that models the number m of muffins based on the time t, in hours, that Julie spends baking.

_____

b. Describe what the rate of change and initial value mean in this situation.

_____

_____

10. The table shows a hot air balloon's height h, in feet, during a descent at various times t, in seconds.

Time (seconds)	Height (feet)
5	1150
10	1090
15	1030
20	970
25	910

a. Use the table's first two ordered pairs to find the hot air balloon's rate of change.

_____

b. Is the rate of change constant? Explain.

_____

_____

c. What was the hot air balloon's height at the time the descent began?

_____

d. Write h as a linear function of t.

_____

11. Jamal owns a computer store. He is tracking his profits from a new computer game he is selling. The table shows Jamal's profits according to how many games were sold.

Games sold	Profit (dollars)
2	−400
4	−360
6	−320
8	−280

He finds the linear function that models his profit p, in dollars, to be $p = \frac{1}{20}g + 22$, where g is the number of computer games sold. His work for finding the rate of change and initial value is shown below.

Rate of change:

$$\frac{4-2}{-360-(-400)} = \frac{2}{40} = \frac{1}{20}$$

Initial value: $p = mg + b$

$$2 = \frac{1}{20}(-400) + b$$
$$2 = -20 + b$$
$$22 = b$$

a. Identify and correct Jamal's error. Write the function that actually models the profit. Show your work.

_____

_____

b. Interpret the rate of change and the initial value found in part a using the fact that profit is the difference between income and expenses.

_____

c. How many games will Jamal need to sell to break even? Explain. Show your work.

_____

_____

8.F.5

SELECTED RESPONSE
Select the correct answer.

1. In the graph of the function, for what values of *x* is *y* increasing?

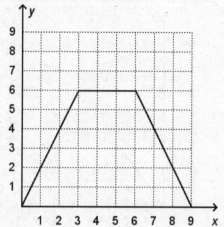

Ⓐ Between *x* = 0 and *x* = 3

Ⓑ Between *x* = 3 and *x* = 6

Ⓒ Between *x* = 6 and *x* = 9

Ⓓ The function is never increasing.

2. What words best describe the function whose graph is shown?

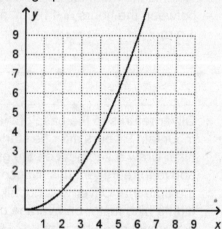

Ⓐ Increasing and linear

Ⓑ Increasing and nonlinear

Ⓒ Decreasing and linear

Ⓓ Decreasing and nonlinear

3. What segment of the graph shows the function having a constant value?

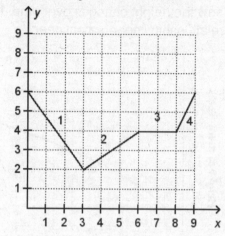

Ⓐ Segment 1   Ⓒ Segment 3

Ⓑ Segment 2   Ⓓ Segment 4

Select all correct answers.

4. What words describe *y* as a function of *x* in the graph below?

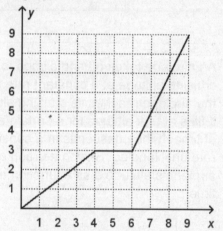

Ⓐ Always increasing

Ⓑ Always decreasing

Ⓒ Constant between *x* = 4 and *x* = 6

Ⓓ Constant between *x* – 0 and *x* – 4

Ⓔ Increasing between *x* = 0 and *x* = 4

Ⓕ Decreasing between *x* = 6 and *x* = 9

Name _____ Date _____ Class _____

CONSTRUCTED RESPONSE

5. The graph below shows the height *h*, in feet, of a plant over *t* months. Describe how the height changes over time. Is the relationship linear or nonlinear?

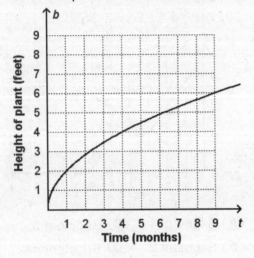

_____

_____

_____

_____

6. An airplane takes off and climbs to its cruising altitude at a constant rate. Once the airplane reaches its cruising altitude, it flies at that altitude for a certain amount of time. It then descends at a constant rate until landing. Sketch a graph of the airplane's altitude *a* as a function of time *t*.

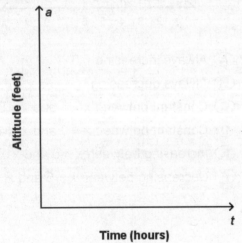

7. Oliver is hiking a trail that takes him straight up a mountain. He starts his hike at 8 a.m. at the base of the mountain. The distance *d*, in miles, that Oliver is from the base of the mountain *t* hours after starting his hike is shown in the graph.

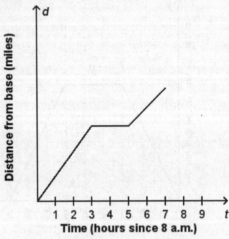

a. Between what times is the slope positive? Interpret the meaning of this in the context of the situation.

_____

_____

b. What is the meaning of the slope between the hours of 11 a.m. and 1 p.m.?

_____

_____

c. Oliver returns to the base of the mountain 9 hours after he started his hike. Draw a segment on the graph above to represent this. Not counting the time that Oliver was not hiking, did he hike faster on average on his way down or on his way up? How do you know?

_____

_____

_____

_____

8.G.1a

SELECTED RESPONSE

Select the correct answer.

1. Point A is located at (−4, 2), and point B is located at (−1, 2). What is the length of the image of $\overline{AB}$ when $\overline{AB}$ is translated 5 units right and 2 units down?

   (A) 2

   (B) 3

   (C) 5

   (D) 8

2. Point A is located at (5, −5), and point B is located at (0, −5). $\overline{AB}$ is rotated counterclockwise 90° about the origin. What are the coordinates of points A′ and B′, the images of points A and B after the rotation?

   (A) A′(−5, 0); B′(−5, −5)

   (B) A′(−5, −5); B′(−5, 0)

   (C) A′(5, 5); B′(5, 0)

   (D) A′(5, 0); B′(5, 5)

3. The graph below shows $\overline{AB}$. What is the length of $\overline{A'B'}$, which is the reflection of $\overline{AB}$ across the y-axis?

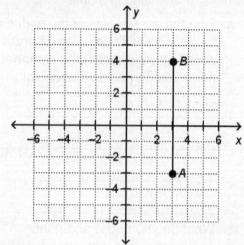

   (A) 1

   (B) 3

   (C) 6

   (D) 7

$\overline{AB}$ has endpoints A(−2, 4) and B(−7, 4). Match each transformation of $\overline{AB}$ with the endpoints of the corresponding image A′B′.

_____ 4. Reflection across x-axis

_____ 5. Reflection across y-axis

_____ 6. Clockwise rotation 90° about the origin

_____ 7. Translation 4 units to the right

_____ 8. Translation 2 units down

A A′(2, 4) and B′(−7, 4)

B A′(2, 4) and B′(−3, 4)

C A′(−2, −4) and B′(−7, −4)

D A′(2, 4) and B′(7, 4)

E A′(−4, −2) and B′(−4, −7)

F A′(−2, 2) and B′(−7, 2)

G A′(−2, 4) and B′(−7, 4)

H A′(4, 2) and B′(4, 7)

Name _____ Date _____ Class _____

CONSTRUCTED RESPONSE

9. The endpoints of $\overline{AB}$ are $A(-8, -3)$ and $B(-5, -3)$. The segment is translated right 3 units, then down 5 units, then left 3 units, and finally up 5 units.

   a. Find the coordinates of the endpoints for each translation using different consecutive letters of the alphabet to name each translated endpoint.

   _____

   _____

   _____

   _____

   b. What do you notice about the coordinates after the last translation?

   _____

10. The graph below shows $\overline{AB}$. Gale rotates $\overline{AB}$ clockwise 90° about the origin and then translates the result 2 units down. He calls this $\overline{A'B'}$, which is also shown on the coordinate plane. Is Gale's work correct? If not, state what transformations Gale must have performed, and then draw the correct transformed segment. What do you notice about the orientation and length of the transformed segment?

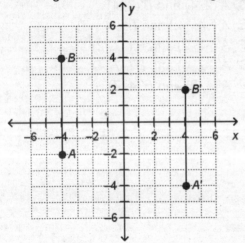

11. $\overleftrightarrow{AB}$ is a horizontal line passing through the point $(0, 3)$. If $\overleftrightarrow{AB}$ is reflected across the x-axis, what point on the y-axis, if any, will it pass through? Is the image of $\overleftrightarrow{AB}$ horizontal, vertical, or neither?

   _____

   _____

12. The equation of $\overleftrightarrow{AB}$ is $x = -2$.

   a. If $\overleftrightarrow{AB}$ is rotated 90° clockwise about the origin, what is the equation of the resulting line?

   _____

   b. If $\overleftrightarrow{AB}$ is rotated 180° clockwise about the origin, what is the equation of the resulting line?

   _____

13. The endpoints of $\overline{AB}$ are $A(-a, -b)$ and $B(-a, c)$ for positive numbers a, b, and c.

   a. What are the endpoints of the image of $\overline{AB}$ after a reflection across the y-axis?

   _____

   b. What are the endpoints of the transformed segment from part a after a 90° counterclockwise rotation about the origin?

   _____

   c. What are the endpoints of the transformed segment from part b after a translation 2a units down?

   _____

   d. For what rotation of $\overline{AB}$ is the image the same as the transformed segment from part c?

   _____

SELECTED RESPONSE
Select the correct answer.

1. In △ABC, m∠A = 40°, m∠B = 90°, and m∠C = 50°. If the triangle is rotated 90° clockwise about a point, what is the measure of the image of ∠A?

   Ⓐ 40°

   Ⓑ 50°

   Ⓒ 90°

   Ⓓ 180°

2. If m∠BAC = 45°, m∠ACB = 72°, and △ABC undergoes the transformation $(x, y) \rightarrow (x, -y)$, what is the measure of the image of ∠ABC?

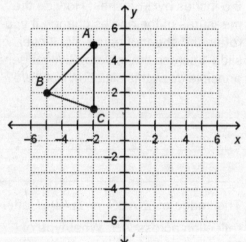

   Ⓐ 45°

   Ⓑ 63°

   Ⓒ 72°

   Ⓓ 180°

3. Quadrilateral WXYZ is the image of quadrilateral ABCD translated 9 units left and 4 units up. If you know m∠A, what other angle do you know the measure of?

   Ⓐ ∠W

   Ⓑ ∠X

   Ⓒ ∠Y

   Ⓓ ∠Z

4. Seth is designing a symmetrical logo for his store. He draws half of the logo, which is shown in the second quadrant below. He then reflects that half of the logo across the y-axis to finish it. Which angle in the reflection has the same measure as ∠A?

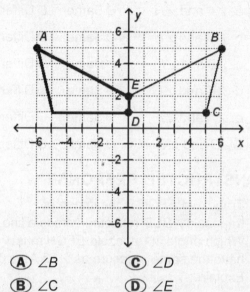

   Ⓐ ∠B   Ⓒ ∠D

   Ⓑ ∠C   Ⓓ ∠E

Select all correct answers.

5. Quadrilateral QRST is the image of quadrilateral ABCD after the transformation $(x, y) \rightarrow (-y, x)$ is applied. Which angles have the same measure?

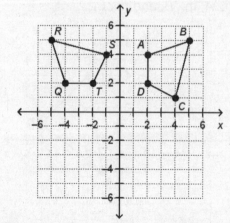

   Ⓐ ∠A and ∠T   Ⓔ ∠A and ∠Q

   Ⓑ ∠D and ∠T   Ⓕ ∠B and ∠S

   Ⓒ ∠B and ∠R   Ⓖ ∠C and ∠S

   Ⓓ ∠C and ∠Q   Ⓗ ∠D and ∠R

Select the correct answer for each lettered part.

6. No two angles of △*ABC* have the same measure. △*FGH* is the image of △*ABC* after being translated 5 units to the right and 8 units down. For each pair of angles, determine whether the angles have the same measure.

   a. ∠*A* and ∠*H*   ○ Same   ○ Different

   b. ∠*C* and ∠*H*   ○ Same   ○ Different

   c. ∠*B* and ∠*F*   ○ Same   ○ Different

   d. ∠*C* and ∠*G*   ○ Same   ○ Different

   e. ∠*A* and ∠*F*   ○ Same   ○ Different

   f. ∠*B* and ∠*G*   ○ Same   ○ Different

CONSTRUCTED RESPONSE

7. Trapezoid *EFGH* is the image of trapezoid *ABCD* reflected across a line. Which angle in trapezoid *EFGH* must have the same measure as ∠*B*? As ∠*C*? Explain.

   _____

8. △*DEF* is the image of △*ABC* after the transformation $(x, y) \rightarrow (-x, y)$. Draw △*DEF* on the coordinate plane and find m∠*D*, m∠*E*, and m∠*F* in terms of m∠*A*, m∠*B*, and m∠*C*.

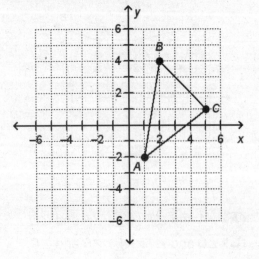

   _____

9. Patricia is painting sailboats on her wall using stencils. The stencil for the sail is a right triangle, △*ABC*, where m∠*A* = 52°, m∠*B* = 90°, and m∠*C* = 38°. Patricia paints one sail on the wall and moves the stencil 8 inches to the right. If she paints a second sail in that spot, what will the measures of the angles be? Let △*A'B'C'* represent the second sail. What general principle does this situation illustrate?

   _____

   _____

   _____

10. Consider a standard sheet of paper, which is a rectangle that measures 8.5 inches by 11 inches. How do the measures of the angles change if you rotate the sheet of paper, flip it over, and slide it across the tabletop? What general principle does this situation illustrate?

    _____

    _____

    _____

11. The image of △*ABC* is △*ABC'* after a reflection across $\overline{AB}$. What type of triangle is △*C'AC*? How does ∠*C'* compare to ∠*C*? How does ∠*C'AC* compare to ∠*BAC*? Justify your answers.

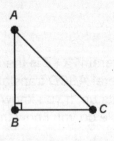

    _____

    _____

    _____

8.G.1c

SELECTED RESPONSE
Select the correct answer.

1. In the regular hexagon shown, the images of which sides are NOT parallel after the hexagon is reflected across the y-axis?

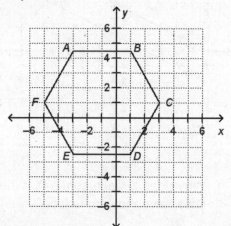

Ⓐ $\overline{AB}$ and $\overline{DE}$

Ⓑ $\overline{EF}$ and $\overline{BC}$

Ⓒ $\overline{CD}$ and $\overline{EF}$

Ⓓ $\overline{AF}$ and $\overline{CD}$

2. A regular octagon is rotated 180° counterclockwise about the origin. How many pairs of sides are parallel in the image?

Ⓐ 1   Ⓒ 3

Ⓑ 2   Ⓓ 4

3. The image of pentagon ABCDE after it is translated right 8 units and up 3 units is pentagon QRSTU. If sides $\overline{BC}$ and $\overline{AE}$ are parallel in ABCDE and there are no other parallel sides, which sides in the image are parallel?

Ⓐ $\overline{RS}$ and $\overline{QU}$

Ⓑ $\overline{QR}$ and $\overline{ST}$

Ⓒ $\overline{RS}$ and $\overline{TU}$

Ⓓ $\overline{ST}$ and $\overline{QU}$

4. Quadrilateral WXYZ is the image of quadrilateral ABCD after it is rotated 90° clockwise about the origin and then translated left 3 units. If sides $\overline{WZ}$ and $\overline{XY}$ are parallel in quadrilateral WXYZ, which sides must be parallel in the original quadrilateral?

Ⓐ $\overline{AB}$ and $\overline{AD}$ Ⓒ $\overline{CD}$ and $\overline{BC}$

Ⓑ $\overline{BC}$ and $\overline{AD}$ Ⓓ $\overline{AB}$ and $\overline{CD}$

Select all correct answers.

5. The translation $(x, y) \rightarrow (x + 12, y)$ is performed on rectangle ABCD drawn on a coordinate plane. Which of the following sides of the image are parallel after the translation?

Ⓐ The images of $\overline{AB}$ and $\overline{BC}$

Ⓑ The images of $\overline{BC}$ and $\overline{CD}$

Ⓒ The images of $\overline{AB}$ and $\overline{CD}$

Ⓓ The images of $\overline{AD}$ and $\overline{CD}$

Ⓔ The images of $\overline{AB}$ and $\overline{AD}$

Ⓕ The images of $\overline{AD}$ and $\overline{BC}$

CONSTRUCTED RESPONSE

6. The transformation $(x, y) \rightarrow (x, -y)$ is performed on rhombus ABCD drawn on a coordinate plane. Which sides of the image are parallel? Explain.

_____

7. Some bookcases have adjustable shelves. If two shelves on such a bookcase are each moved up 2 inches, are they still parallel? Would they still be parallel if they were moved down 2 inches instead? What does this illustrate about vertical translations of parallel lines?

_____

_____

8. Lines *a* and *b* are horizontal and therefore parallel. Reflect these lines across the *x*-axis. What can you say about the images of lines *a* and *b*?

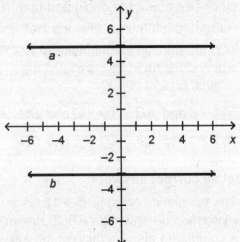

_____

9. Rectangle *ABCD* is shown.

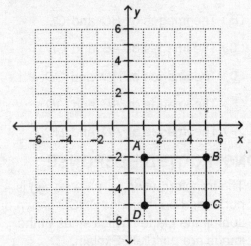

a. Which pairs of sides of the rectangle are parallel?

_____

b. The translation $(x, y) \rightarrow (x - 4, y + 7)$ is applied to *ABCD*. On the coordinate plane above, draw the image of *ABCD* and label it as *A'B'C'D'*.

c. What pairs of sides from *A'B'C'D'* are parallel? Explain.

_____

10. Lines *m* and *n*, shown below, are parallel. The equations of lines *m* and *n* are

$$y = \frac{1}{2}x + 3 \quad \text{and} \quad y = \frac{1}{2}x + 1, \text{ respectively.}$$

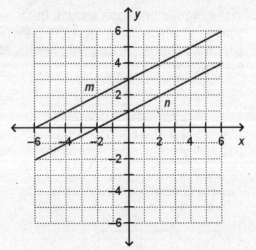

a. Why does it make sense that the lines have the same slope?

_____

b. Line *m'* is the image of line *m* after the transformation $(x, y) \rightarrow (x, -y)$. Draw *n'*, the image of line *n* after the same transformation.

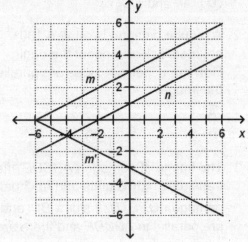

c. What are the equations of line *m'* and line *n'*?

_____

d. Are lines *m'* and *n'* parallel? Explain.

_____

SELECTED RESPONSE
Select the correct answer.

1. Figure A is congruent to figure B. What sequence of transformations maps figure A to figure B?

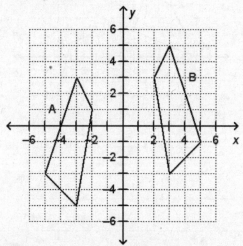

Ⓐ $(x, y) \rightarrow (x, -y)$ followed by $(x, y) \rightarrow (x, y + 2)$

Ⓑ $(x, y) \rightarrow (-x, y)$ followed by $(x, y) \rightarrow (x, y + 2)$

Ⓒ $(x, y) \rightarrow (x, y - 2)$ followed by $(x, y) \rightarrow (-x, y)$

Ⓓ $(x, y) \rightarrow (x, y - 2)$ followed by $(x, y) \rightarrow (x, -y)$

2. Which set of vertices describes a triangle that is the result of performing a sequence of translations, reflections, and/or rotations on the triangle with vertices $(-5, 2)$, $(-2, 2)$, $(-3, 6)$ and is therefore congruent to the triangle?

Ⓐ $(2, 2)$, $(3, 6)$, $(6, 2)$

Ⓑ $(-6, -1)$, $(-6, -4)$, $(-2, -3)$

Ⓒ $(0, 0)$, $(3, 0)$, $(2, 3)$

Ⓓ $(2, -1)$, $(5, -2)$, $(3, -6)$

Select all correct answers.

3. Which sequences of transformations map triangle A to triangle B, thereby showing that the triangles are congruent?

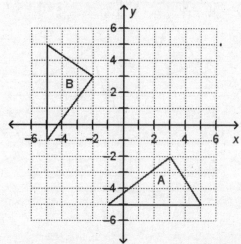

Ⓐ Reflect across the x-axis, and then rotate 90° counterclockwise about the origin.

Ⓑ Reflect across the y-axis, and then rotate 90° counterclockwise about the origin.

Ⓒ Reflect across the x-axis, and then rotate 90° clockwise about the origin.

Ⓓ Reflect across the y-axis, and then rotate 90° clockwise about the origin.

Ⓔ Reflect across the x-axis, and then rotate 180° counterclockwise about the origin.

Ⓕ Reflect across the y-axis, and then rotate 180° counterclockwise about the origin.

CONSTRUCTED RESPONSE

4. Is $\triangle ABC \cong \triangle DEF$? If so, give a sequence of transformations that maps $\triangle ABC$ to $\triangle DEF$. If not, explain.

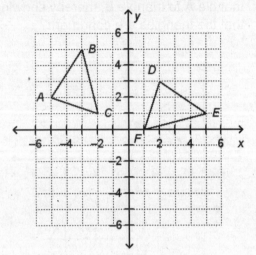

_____

_____

5. Decide if each set of vertices forms a figure that is congruent to the given figure. Use transformations to explain your answers.

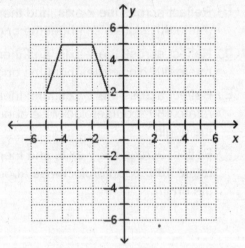

  a. (5, –2), (4, 1), (2, 1), (1, –2)

_____

_____

  b. (4, 1), (3, 4), (1, 4), (0, 3)

_____

_____

6. Are quadrilaterals $ABCD$ and $WXYZ$ congruent? If so, give a sequence of transformations that maps $ABCD$ to $WXYZ$. If not, explain.

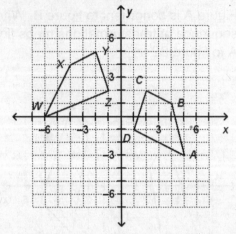

_____

_____

7. The vertices of a quadrilateral are (1, 2), (3, 1), (2, 4), and (5, 3). Draw the figure on the coordinate plane. Perform the following transformations, where each transformation is applied to the previous image. Draw each image on the coordinate plane, keeping track of which transformation was performed. Are the original figure and final image congruent? Explain.

  a. $(x, y) \rightarrow (x - 3, y + 1)$

  b. $(x, y) \rightarrow (-y, x)$

  c. $(x, y) \rightarrow (-x, y)$

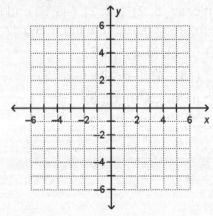

_____

_____

8.G.3

SELECTED RESPONSE
Select all correct answers.

1. The rectangle shown is translated 6 units to the left. Which ordered pair is NOT a vertex of the image?

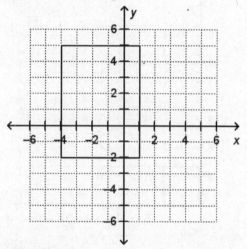

Ⓐ (2, –2)

Ⓑ (–10, 5)

Ⓒ (–5, –2)

Ⓓ (–5, 5)

2. Figure B is the image of figure A under what transformation?

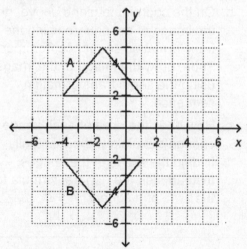

Ⓐ (x, y) → (x, y – 4)

Ⓑ (x, y) → (–x, y)

Ⓒ (x, y) → (x, –y)

Ⓓ (x, y) → (x, y – 7)

3. Figure B is the image of figure A after a dilation centered at the origin. What is the scale factor of the dilation?

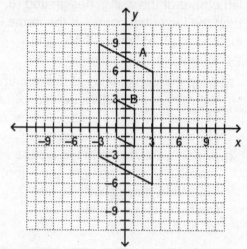

Ⓐ $\frac{1}{3}$ Ⓒ 1

Ⓑ $\frac{1}{2}$ Ⓓ 3

Select all correct answers.

4. The figure shown is rotated 180° clockwise about the origin. Which ordered pairs are the vertices of the image?

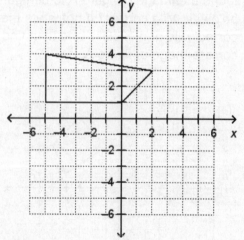

Ⓐ (5, –4)   Ⓓ (0, –1)

Ⓑ (5, –1)   Ⓔ (3, –2)

Ⓒ (1, 5)   Ⓕ (–2, –3)

Name _____ Date _____ Class _____

CONSTRUCTED RESPONSE

5. Vince is moving a rectangular picture frame on a wall. The picture frame is 2 feet long and 1 foot tall. If the bottom left corner of the wall is designated (0, 0), then the lower left corner of the frame is located at (3, 5), where the *x*- and *y*-coordinates are measured in feet.

   a. Find the coordinates of the remaining corners of the picture frame.

   _____

   b. Vince wants to move the picture frame 2 feet to the right and 1 foot up. Write a symbolic rule that represents the transformation.

   _____

   c. Find the coordinates of each corner of the frame after Vince moves the frame.

   _____

6. Mila claims that the image of a figure reflected across the *x*-axis and translated 2 units down is given by the rule $(x, y) \rightarrow (-x, y - 2)$. Using this rule, Mila found the image of figure A to be figure B below. Is Mila correct? If not, state the correct rule and explain, and then find the correct image of figure A.

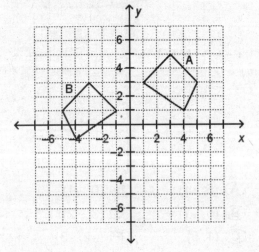

7. Rosa is making a pattern using the square with side length 4 units shown below. The square undergoes a dilation with a scale factor of $\frac{3}{2}$ centered at the origin, followed by a translation 4 units up and 4 units right.

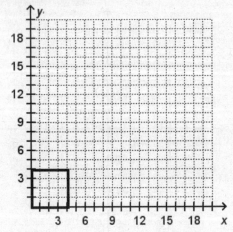

   a. Write symbolic rules for the two transformations that Rosa uses to create her pattern using the given square.

   _____

   _____

   b. On the coordinate plane above, draw the image of the square using the transformation sequence from part a. Then, draw the image of the image using the same transformation sequence.

   c. How does the area of each image change? Explain without actually finding the areas of the images. Instead, use the general formula for the area of a square, $A = s^2$.

   _____

   _____

   _____

   _____

   _____

SELECTED RESPONSE
Select the correct answer.

1. Which set of vertices forms a figure that is similar but NOT congruent to the figure shown?

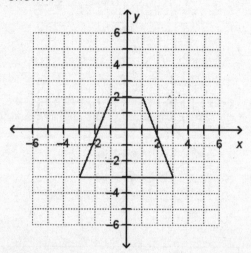

- Ⓐ (−3, 3), (2, 1), (2, −1), (−3, −3)
- Ⓑ (−6, −6), (−2, 4), (2, 4), (6, −6)
- Ⓒ (−2, −6), (0, −1), (2, −1), (4, −6)
- Ⓓ (−3, 3), (−1, −2), (1, −2), (3, 3)

2. Which sequence of transformations maps rectangle *ABCD* to rectangle *WXYZ* and shows that *ABCD* ~ *WXYZ*?

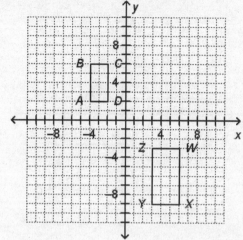

- Ⓐ (x, y) → (x + 4, y − 4) followed by (x, y) → (1.5x, 1.5y)
- Ⓑ (x, y) → (1.5x + 1.5y) followed by (x, y) → (x + 9, y − 6)
- Ⓒ (x, y) → (−x, −y) followed by (x, y) → (1.5x, 1.5y)
- Ⓓ (x, y) → (1.5x, 1.5y) followed by (x, y) → (−x, y)

Select the correct answer for each lettered part.

3. Identify which sequences of transformations performed on the figure shown result in a similar but NOT congruent figure or a similar and congruent figure.

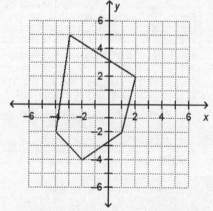

a. (x, y) → (x − 3, y + 8) followed by (x, y) → (y, −x)
  ○ Similar and not congruent   ○ Similar and congruent

b. (x, y) → (−x, y) followed by (x, y) → (5x, 5y)
  ○ Similar and not congruent   ○ Similar and congruent

c. (x, y) → (x, −y) followed by (x, y) → (x − 3, y)
  ○ Similar and not congruent   ○ Similar and congruent

d. (x, y) → (0.1x, 0.1y) followed by (x, y) → (−y, x)
  ○ Similar and not congruent   ○ Similar and congruent

CONSTRUCTED RESPONSE

4. Is △ABC ~ △DEF? If so, give a sequence of transformations that maps △ABC to △DEF. If not, explain.

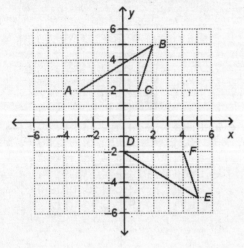

_____

_____

_____

5. ABCD and QRST are parallelograms. Is ABCD ~ QRST? Explain.

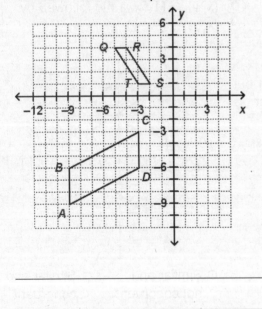

_____

_____

_____

6. Callie claims that figure 1 and figure 2 are neither congruent nor similar. Is Callie's claim correct? If so, explain. If not, find a sequence of transformations that maps figure 1 to figure 2 and shows that they are congruent, similar, or both.

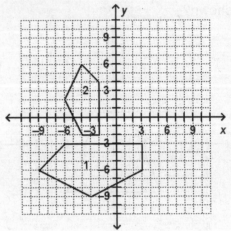

_____

_____

_____

7. a. Figure A and figure B are similar. Figure B is the image of figure A after a dilation with respect to the origin by a scale factor of k followed by a reflection across the x-axis. Prove that these transformations can also be done in the reverse order to map figure A to figure B.

_____

_____

   b. Figure C and figure D are similar. Figure D is the image of figure C after a dilation with respect to the origin by a scale factor of k followed by a translation right a units. Prove that these transformations must be done in this particular order to map figure C to figure D.

_____

_____

SELECTED RESPONSE

Select the correct answer.

1. In the triangle, m∠1 = 42° and m∠4 = 81°. What is m∠2?

    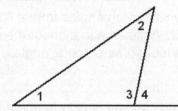

    (A) 39°

    (B) 42°

    (C) 99°

    (D) 123°

2. Which of the following guarantees that △ABC and △DEF are similar triangles?

    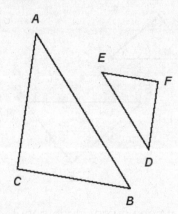

    (A) ∠B ≅ ∠E, and $\overline{BC} ≅ \overline{EF}$

    (B) ∠C ≅ ∠F, and $\overline{AC} ≅ \overline{DF}$

    (C) ∠B ≅ ∠E, and ∠C ≅ ∠F

    (D) $\overline{BC} ≅ \overline{EF}$, and $\overline{AC} ≅ \overline{DF}$

3. Which set of angles does NOT form a triangle?

    (A) 85°, 43°, and 52°

    (B) 90°, 37°, and 51°

    (C) 37°, 65°, and 78°

    (D) 120°, 12°, and 48°

4. △ABC and △DEF are similar triangles. If m∠A = 104° and m∠E = 36°, what is m∠C?

    (A) 36°

    (B) 40°

    (C) 76°

    (D) 104°

Select all correct answers.

5. Suppose two parallel lines are cut by a transversal. What angle relationships describe congruent angles in this context?

    (A) Corresponding angles

    (B) Linear pair

    (C) Same-side interior angles

    (D) Same-side exterior angles

    (E) Alternate exterior angles

    (F) Alternate interior angles

CONSTRUCTED RESPONSE

6. Parallel lines a and b are cut by the transversal t. Explain how transformations can be used to show that ∠4 ≅ ∠8 and ∠4 ≅ ∠5.

    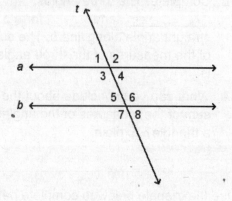

    _____

    _____

    _____

    _____

    _____

7. Use the figure shown to complete parts a through e, which constitute a proof of the triangle sum theorem.

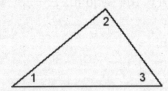

a. Draw line *a* through the base of the triangle. Draw line *b* through the vertex opposite the base and parallel to line *a*.

b. Extend the other two sides of the triangle in both directions. Label the left line *t* and the right line *s*. These two lines intersect the parallel lines *a* and *b* and are called _____.

c. Two acute angles adjacent to ∠2 are formed by lines *t*, *s*, and *b*. Label the left angle ∠4 and the right angle ∠5. Complete the following statements:

∠1 and _____ are one pair of alternate interior angles; ∠3 and _____ are another pair of alternate interior angles. The angles in each pair of alternate interior angles are _____.

d. Complete: The three angles, _____, _____, and _____, form a straight angle along line *b*. The sum of the measures of the three angles is _____.

e. What can you conclude about the sum of the measures of the angles of a triangle? Explain.

_____

8. Use the triangle below to complete parts a through d, which constitute a proof of the exterior angle theorem.

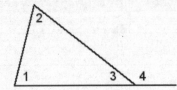

a. Identify the exterior angle and the remote interior angles.

_____

b. Complete using the triangle sum theorem: ____ + ____ + ____ = 180°.

c. Identify which angles form a linear pair. Write an equation for the sum of the measures of these angles.

_____

d. What can you conclude about the measures of an exterior angle and its remote interior angles? Justify your conclusion by using the information from parts a through c.

_____

9. In the triangles below, ∠A ≅ ∠D and ∠B ≅ ∠E.

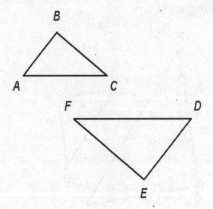

a. What can you conclude about ∠C and ∠F? Explain.

_____

b. Can you conclude that △ABC and △DEF are similar? Explain your reasoning without using the angle-angle similarity criterion.

_____

c. Can you conclude that △ABC and △DEF are congruent? Explain your reasoning.

_____

8.G.6

SELECTED RESPONSE
Select the correct answer.

1. The diagram below is used to prove the Pythagorean theorem. What expression represents the length of a side of the larger square in the diagram?

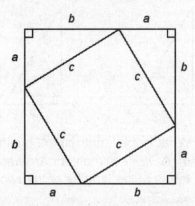

- (A) c
- (B) $a + b$
- (C) $a - b$
- (D) $b - a$

2. The diagram below is used to prove the Pythagorean theorem. What is the area of the trapezoid in the diagram?

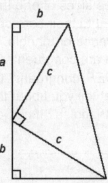

- (A) $\frac{1}{2}(a+b)(b+c)$
- (B) $\frac{1}{2}(a-b)(a+b)$
- (C) $(a+b)^2$
- (D) $\frac{1}{2}(a+b)^2$

3. Suppose you know the following facts about $\triangle ABC$ and $\triangle DEF$:

   (1) Both triangles have sides of length a and b.

   (2) For $\triangle ABC$, $a^2 + b^2 = c^2$.

   (3) For $\triangle DEF$, $\angle F$ is a right angle.

   What can be said about the value of c in $\triangle ABC$ and the length of the hypotenuse of $\triangle DEF$?

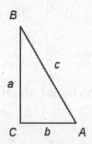 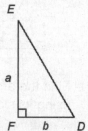

- (A) The value of c in $\triangle ABC$ is $\sqrt{a^2+b^2}$, and the length of the hypotenuse of $\triangle DEF$ is $a^2 + b^2$.
- (B) The value of c in $\triangle ABC$ is $a^2 + b^2$, and the length of the hypotenuse of $\triangle DEF$ is $\sqrt{a^2+b^2}$.
- (C) The value of c in $\triangle ABC$ is $\sqrt{a^2+b^2}$, and the length of the hypotenuse of $\triangle DEF$ is $\sqrt{a^2+b^2}$.
- (D) The value of c in $\triangle ABC$ is $a^2 + b^2$, and the length of the hypotenuse of $\triangle DEF$ is $a^2 + b^2$.

CONSTRUCTED RESPONSE

4. A square is decomposed into four congruent right triangles and one smaller square as shown. Use the diagram to complete parts a–c, which constitute a proof of the Pythagorean theorem.

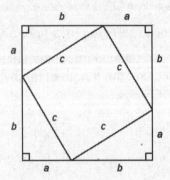

   a. Find the area of the larger square using its side length.

   _____

   b. Find the combined area of the four triangles and the smaller square.

   _____

   c. Set the expressions from parts a and b equal to each other. Simplify.

   _____

5. Three right triangles are arranged to form a trapezoid as shown. Use the area of the trapezoid and the combined area of the triangles to prove the Pythagorean theorem.

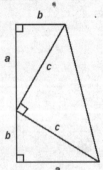

   _____

   _____

6. Suppose that for $\triangle ABC$ shown below, $a^2 + b^2 = c^2$. Also shown is $\triangle DEF$, which is a right triangle whose two legs have lengths a and b and whose hypotenuse has length f. Prove the converse of the Pythagorean theorem by completing parts a–d.

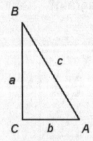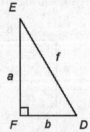

   a. What is the length of the hypotenuse of $\triangle DEF$? Write your answer in terms of the lengths of the two legs of $\triangle DEF$.

   _____

   b. What can you say about the side of length c in $\triangle ABC$ and the hypotenuse of $\triangle DEF$? Explain.

   _____

   _____

   c. If all three sides of one triangle are congruent to their corresponding sides in another triangle, then the triangles are congruent. Are $\triangle ABC$ and $\triangle DEF$ congruent? If so, what does that tell you about the angles of the two triangles? If not, explain.

   _____

   _____

   d. What can you conclude about $\triangle ABC$? Explain.

   _____

   _____

8.G.7

SELECTED RESPONSE
Select the correct answer.

1. What is the unknown side length, to the nearest tenth of a meter, in the triangle shown?

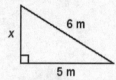

Ⓐ 1.0 m
Ⓑ 3.3 m
Ⓒ 7.8 m
Ⓓ 11.0 m

2. The size of a computer screen is measured along the diagonal. What is the approximate size, measured to the nearest inch, of a 12 in. by 10.5 in. computer screen?

Ⓐ 6 in.
Ⓑ 16 in.
Ⓒ 23 in.
Ⓓ 254 in.

3. What is the approximate length of the diagonal from point A to point B in the right rectangular prism shown? Round your answer to the nearest centimeter.

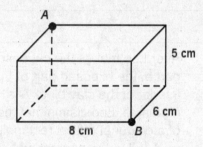

Ⓐ 8 cm
Ⓑ 9 cm
Ⓒ 10 cm
Ⓓ 11 cm

Select all correct answers.

4. Which measurements, rounded to the nearest tenth of a yard, are the unknown lengths in the figure shown?

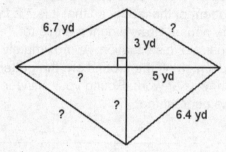

Ⓐ 4.0 yd
Ⓑ 5.8 yd
Ⓒ 6.0 yd
Ⓓ 7.2 yd
Ⓔ 7.3 yd
Ⓕ 8.1 yd

5. Which measurements, rounded to the nearest tenth of a yard, are the lengths of a diagonal of the right rectangular prism or any diagonal of a face of the prism?

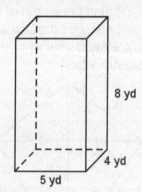

Ⓐ 6.2 yd
Ⓑ 6.4 yd
Ⓒ 8.9 yd
Ⓓ 9.4 yd
Ⓔ 10.2 yd
Ⓕ 12.0 yd

CONSTRUCTED RESPONSE

6. Maurice is cleaning out the rain gutters on his house. To get to the gutters, he places a 24 ft ladder against the house so that the top of the ladder reaches the bottom of the gutters. He places the bottom of the ladder so that it is 7 ft from the house. Draw a right triangle to illustrate this situation. Approximately how high off the ground are the gutters? Show your work. Round your answer to the nearest foot.

_____

_____

_____

7. Manuel is making a kite. He cuts out a piece of cloth in the shape shown. He uses two sticks as supports. The vertical stick is 90 cm long, and the horizontal stick is 80 cm long. They intersect at a right angle 60 cm from the bottom of the vertical stick. The vertical stick bisects the horizontal stick, as shown. Manuel wants to add a border around the perimeter of the kite. What is the length of material Manuel will need for the border? Show your work. Round your answer to the nearest centimeter.

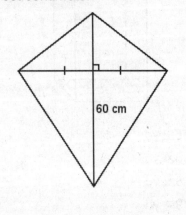

_____

_____

_____

8. What is the approximate area of △ABC? Show your work. Round your answer to the nearest tenth of a square centimeter.

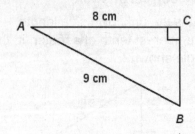

_____

_____

9. Leo is cutting a clay block in the shape of a right rectangular prism. The dimensions of the block are shown.

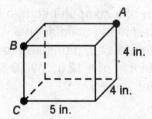

a. Leo claims that if he cuts vertically downward between points A and B, the approximate length of the cut from point A to point B, rounded to the nearest inch, is 6 in. Is Leo correct? Explain. If he is not correct, find the correct approximate length.

_____

_____

b. After Leo makes the cut described in part a, the exposed part of the interior of the clay block is a rectangle. Leo claims that the length of a diagonal of that rectangle, rounded to the nearest inch, is 7 in. Is Leo correct? Explain. If he is not correct, find the correct approximate length.

_____

_____

8.G.8

SELECTED RESPONSE
Select the correct answer.

1. Find the length of $\overline{AB}$ in $\triangle ABC$ shown on the coordinate plane. Round to the nearest unit.

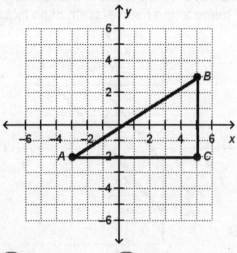

(A) 5   (C) 9

(B) 8   (D) 13

2. Every morning, Cho rides his bicycle from his house to the park and then back to his house. He takes the same route in both directions. His route is shown on the coordinate plane, where each unit represents 1 mile. How far does Cho ride every morning? Round to the nearest tenth of a mile.

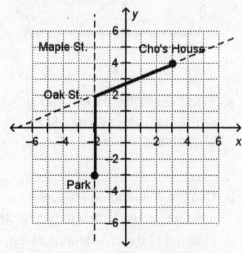

(A) 5.0 miles   (C) 10.4 miles

(B) 5.4 miles   (D) 20.8 miles

3. Find the perimeter of the square shown. Round to the nearest tenth.

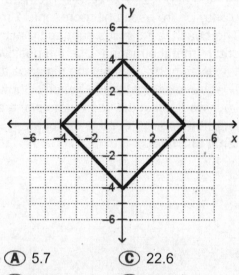

(A) 5.7   (C) 22.6

(B) 16.0   (D) 32.0

Use the coordinate plane to match each segment with its corresponding length rounded to the nearest tenth.

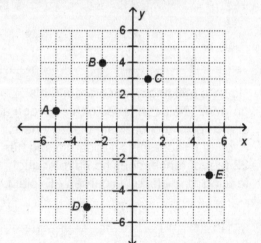

_____ 4. $\overline{AB}$ **A** 3.2

_____ 5. $\overline{CE}$ **B** 4.2

_____ 6. $\overline{BE}$ **C** 7.2

_____ 7. $\overline{BD}$ **D** 8.2

_____ 8. $\overline{CD}$ **E** 8.9

                              F 9.1

                              G 9.9

                              H 10.8

CONSTRUCTED RESPONSE

9. A boat travels a straight route from the marina to the beach. The marina is located at point (0, 0) on a coordinate plane, where each unit represents 1 mile. The beach is 3.5 miles east and 4 miles south from the marina. Use the positive y-axis as north. What is the distance the boat travels to get to the beach? Show your work using the coordinate plane and a right triangle. Round to the nearest tenth of a mile.

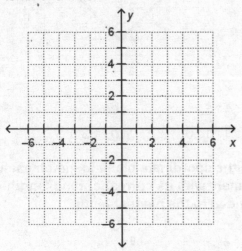

10. Noah is building a fence around his garden. The boundaries of his garden are shown on the coordinate plane, where each unit represents 1 foot. If Noah has 22 feet of fence, does he have enough fencing to enclose his garden? Explain.

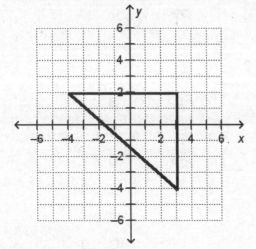

11. Jeffrey is making a new post for his mail box using three pieces of wood. Two of the pieces will form a right angle. The third piece will be used as a support for the mailbox, as shown on the coordinate plane below. If each unit represents 1 inch, what is the shortest piece of wood Jeffrey can use to make the support? Round to the nearest tenth of an inch.

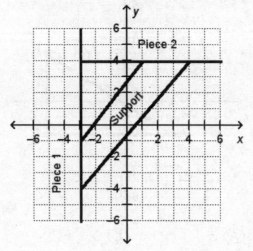

12. The endpoints of $\triangle ABC$ are located at $A(x_1, y_1)$, $B(x_2, y_2)$, and $C(x_2, y_1)$.

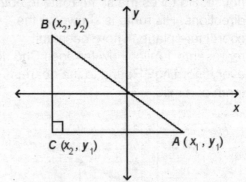

a. Find the lengths of $\overline{AC}$ and $\overline{BC}$ in terms of the coordinates of their endpoints. Explain.

b. Use the Pythagorean theorem to write a formula for the length of $\overline{AB}$ in terms of the coordinates of the endpoints of $\overline{AC}$ and $\overline{BC}$.

8.G.9

SELECTED RESPONSE
Select the correct answer.

1. What is the volume of the cone with the given dimensions? Use 3.14 for π. Round your answer to the nearest tenth of a cubic inch.

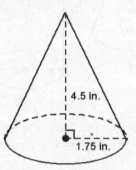

4.5 in.

1.75 in.

Ⓐ 8.25 in³   Ⓒ 43.3 in³

Ⓑ 14.4 in³   Ⓓ 57.7 in³

2. What is the formula for the volume of a sphere with diameter *d*?

Ⓐ $V = \frac{1}{3}\pi\left(\frac{d}{2}\right)^3$

Ⓑ $V = 4\pi d^3$

Ⓒ $V = \frac{4}{3}\pi\left(\frac{d}{2}\right)^3$

Ⓓ $V = \frac{4}{3}\pi d^3$

3. What is the ratio of the volumes of a cylinder and a cone having the same base radius *r* and height *h*?

Ⓐ The volume of a cone is 3 times the volume of a cylinder.

Ⓑ The volume of a cylinder is 3 times the volume of a cone.

Ⓒ The volume of a cylinder is $\frac{1}{3}$ times the volume of a cone.

Ⓓ The volumes of a cylinder and a cone are equal.

4. A cylindrical soup can has a height of $3\frac{1}{2}$ in. and a diameter of $2\frac{1}{8}$ in. What is the volume of the soup can? Use 3.14 for π. Round to the nearest tenth of a cubic inch.

Ⓐ 4.1 in³

Ⓑ 12.4 in³

Ⓒ 23.4 in³

Ⓓ 49.6 in³

5. A ball has a radius of 8 cm. What is the volume of the ball? Use 3.14 for π. Round to the nearest tenth of a cubic centimeter.

Ⓐ 267.9 cm³

Ⓑ 535.9 cm³

Ⓒ 1,607.7 cm³

Ⓓ 2,143.6 cm³

Select all correct answers.

6. Stefan is making a two-tier cake in the shape shown. The diameter of the bottom cylindrical tier is 8 in., and the diameter of the top cylindrical tier is 5 in. Which measurements are the volumes of each tier and the entire cake? Use 3.14 for π. Round to the nearest cubic inch.

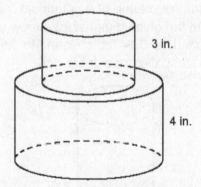

3 in.

4 in.

Ⓐ 59 in³   Ⓓ 260 in³

Ⓑ 201 in³   Ⓔ 804 in³

Ⓒ 236 in³   Ⓕ 1,040 in³

CONSTRUCTED RESPONSE

7. The radius of a softball is 3.75 cm, and the radius of a table tennis ball is 2 cm. The volume of the softball is how many times greater than the volume of the table tennis ball? Show your work using ratios. Use 3.14 for π. Round to the nearest tenth.

_____

8. Tyler's basketball team just won the state championship. The trophy is a silver basketball sitting on top of a cylindrical wooden base. The basketball has a radius of 2.35 in. The base has a radius equal to that of the basketball and a height of 2 in. Find the total volume of the trophy. Show your work. Use 3.14 for π. Round to the nearest tenth of a cubic inch.

_____

9. The sharpened end of a round pencil has a height of 15 mm and a base diameter of 5 mm. The rest of the pencil has a height of 175 mm. What is the total volume of the pencil? Show your work. Use 3.14 for π.

_____

10. Find the volume of a cylindrical candle with the given dimensions. Show your work. Use 3.14 for π. Round to the nearest tenth of a cubic inch.

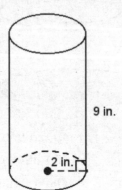

9 in.

2 in.

11. A cone and a cylinder have the given dimensions. Assume the cone is placed inside the cylinder.

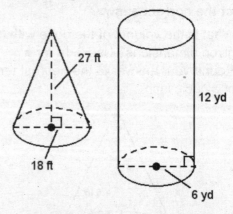

27 ft

18 ft

12 yd

6 yd

a. Explain why the cone and cylinder have the same base radius.

_____

b. Find a general formula to find the remaining volume of the cylinder when the cone has base radius r and height h_1, the cylinder has radius r and height h_2, and r, h_1, and h_2 are measured in the same units.

_____

c. Use your formula from part b to calculate the remaining volume for the cone and cylinder shown. Show your work. Use 3.14 for π.

_____

d. Discuss how your formula from part b changes if the cone and the cylinder have the same base radius and the same height. What do you notice about the remaining volume of the cylinder?

_____

_____

SELECTED RESPONSE
Select the correct answer.

1. Which phrase *best* describes the pattern of association between the variables *x* and *y* shown in the scatter plot?

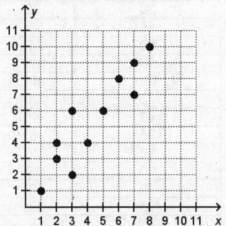

(A) A positive, linear association

(B) A negative, linear association

(C) A positive, nonlinear association

(D) No association

2. The scatter plot shows the number of pitches a baseball team's starting pitcher throws each game during one season. Which point, if any, is an outlier?

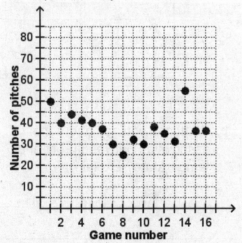

(A) (1, 50)

(B) (8, 25)

(C) (14, 55)

(D) No outliers

3. Which statement *best* describes any clusters there are in the data displayed in the scatter plot shown?

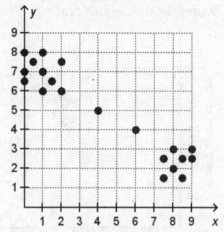

(A) The data cluster around (1, 7).

(B) The data cluster around (8.5, 2).

(C) The data cluster around (1, 7) and (8.5, 2).

(D) There are no clusters.

Select all correct answers.

4. Which phrases *best* describe the pattern of association between the variables *x* and *y* shown in the scatter plot?

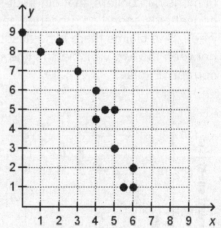

(A) Positive association

(B) Negative association

(C) No association

(D) Linear association

(E) Nonlinear association.

CONSTRUCTED RESPONSE

5. Nadia's English class took a two-part exam. The scatter plot shows the scores for the first part of the exam and the scores for the second part.

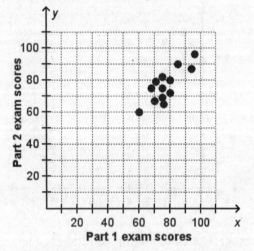

a. Describe the pattern of association.

_____

b. Did students tend to do better, worse, or the same on part 2 of the exam than they did on part 1? Explain.

_____

6. Sydney made a scatter plot of the amount of money, in dollars, that different-sized households spend on groceries each week. She claims there is no association between the two variables. Is she correct? Explain.

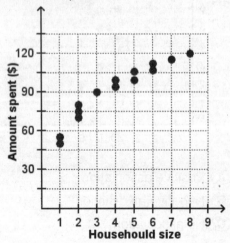

7. Calvin owns a small ice cream stand. His daily profit, in dollars, and the daily maximum temperature, in degrees Fahrenheit, for two weeks during the summer are shown in the table.

Temperature (°F)	Profit ($)
90	160
80	100
65	50
60	20
90	160
100	160
75	100
60	40
95	140
90	130
90	110
70	80
85	90
85	100

a. Make a scatter plot of the data, with temperature along the horizontal axis and profit along the vertical axis.

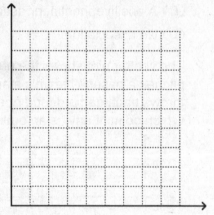

b. What can you say about the association between profit and temperature? Explain.

_____

_____

_____

SELECTED RESPONSE
Select the correct answer.

1. The scatter plot shows the data for the number of hours Grace jogs each week for 8 weeks and the number of miles she jogs. What is the slope of a trend line for the data?

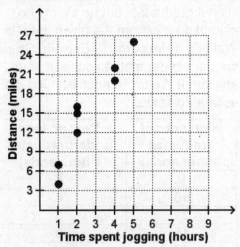

Ⓐ Positive

Ⓑ Negative

Ⓒ Zero

Ⓓ There is no trend line for the data.

2. Which of the following lines *best* fits the data shown in the scatter plot?

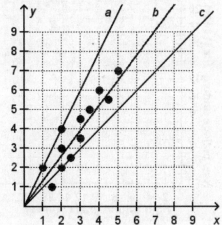

Ⓐ Line *a*

Ⓑ Line *b*

Ⓒ Line *c*

Ⓓ None of the lines fit the data well.

Select all correct answers.

3. Which statements *best* describe the line and its fit to the data points shown?

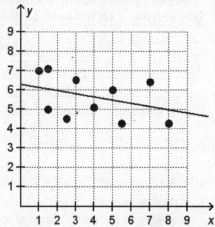

Ⓐ The line fits the data well because it follows the general trend of the data, which is positive and linear.

Ⓑ The line fits the data well because it follows the general trend of the data, which is negative and linear.

Ⓒ The line does not fit the data well because it does not follow the general trend of the data.

Ⓓ There are about an equal number of data points above and below the line, so it fits the data well.

Ⓔ There are about an equal number of data points above and below the line, so it does not fit the data well.

Ⓕ The points are close to the line, so there is a strong linear association between the values of *x* and *y*.

Ⓖ The points are far from the line, so there is a weak linear association between the values of *x* and *y*.

CONSTRUCTED RESPONSE

4. The table shows the number of people in a household and the household's monthly water bill, in hundreds of dollars.

People in household	Monthly water bill (hundreds of dollars)
2	1
1	0.25
5	2.5
6	3.5
4	1.8
1	0.45
2	0.75
5	3

a. Graph the data given in the table, with the number of people per household on the horizontal axis and the water bill on the vertical axis. Describe the relationship between the two variables.

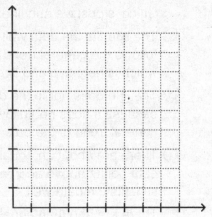

_____

_____

b. Draw a trend line for the data. Is your trend line a good fit? Explain.

_____

_____

c. Estimate the size of a household if the water bill is $150.

_____

5. Walter is comparing the number of high school graduates, in thousands, in his state each spring over the past 11 years and the number of new college undergraduates, in thousands, at a public university in his state each fall. The data are shown in the table. Walter wants to estimate the number of new college undergraduates if there are 13,000 high school graduates, but he claims he cannot do this from the given data. Is Walter's claim correct? Explain. Graph the data in the table to support your answer. If Walter is incorrect, find the estimated value.

High school graduates (thousands)	New college undergraduates (thousands)
9	6
10	6
12	8
15	9
15	10
16	10
17	14
18	14
18	13
18	15
19	15

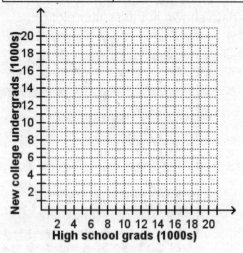

_____

_____

_____

_____

Name _____ Date _____ Class _____

8.SP.3

SELECTED RESPONSE
Select the correct answer.

1. The scatter plot shows the amount of gasoline g, in gallons, in a car's fuel tank and the distance traveled d, in miles, after filling the tank. The equation of a trend line is $g = -\dfrac{1}{30}d + 16$. How much gas is in the fuel tank when it is full?

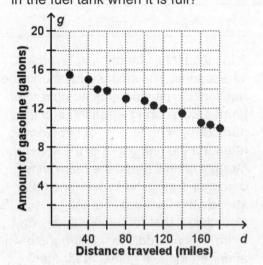

A 10 gallons   **C** 16 gallons

B 15 gallons   **D** 30 gallons

2. Ms. Jackson asked each of her students how much time t, in hours, they studied for the test. She paired these numbers with the students' test scores s and created the scatter plot shown. The equation of the trend line is $s = 9t + 50$. On average, how does a student's score change for each additional hour of studying?

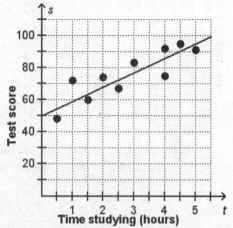

A Decreases by 9 points

B Increases by 9 points

C Decreases by 50 points

D Increases by 50 points

The scatter plot shows the temperature T, in degrees Fahrenheit, recorded on a particular day at various times t, in hours since 6:00 a.m. The equation of the trend line is $T = 4.3t + 21$. Use the trend line to match each description with its value.

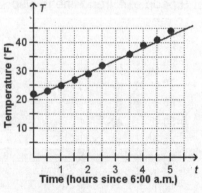

_____ 3. The temperature at 6:00 a.m.

_____ 4. The time, to the nearest half hour, at which the temperature reached freezing (32 °F)

_____ 5. The temperature at 9:00 a.m.

_____ 6. The increase in temperature each hour

_____ 7. The time, to the nearest half hour, at which the temperature will reach 47 °F

A 4.3 °F

B 21 °F

C 33.9 °F

D 47 °F

E 6:00 a.m.

F 8:30 a.m.

G 11:30 a.m.

H Noon (12:00 p.m.)

CONSTRUCTED RESPONSE

8. The scatter plot shows the relationship between the number a of full-page ads in a magazine and the number p of pages in each issue for 12 issues of the magazine. What percent of the pages are full-page ads? Explain.

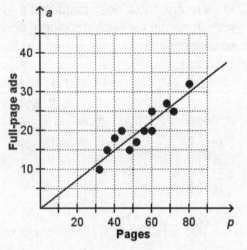

_____

_____

9. The scatter plot shows the relationship between the average number of times t a person goes to a movie theater per month and the person's age a, in years, for 9 people. A trend line is also shown.

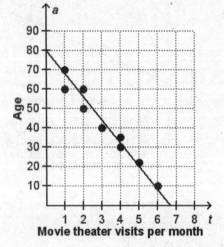

a. What is the equation of the trend line? Show your work.

_____

_____

b. Interpret the constants in the equation of the trend line.

_____

_____

c. Use the equation of the trend line to predict the age of a person who on average goes to a movie theater 3 times per month. Show your work.

_____

_____

10. A local baseball team has played for 11 seasons. The scatter plot shows the relationship between the number w of games won during a season and the number p, in hundreds, of people who attended the last game of the season. Morgan claims that if the team wins 0 games during the season, no one attends the final game of the season. She also claims that for every game won, there was an additional 300 people who attended the last game. Is Morgan correct? Explain using the equation of the trend line.

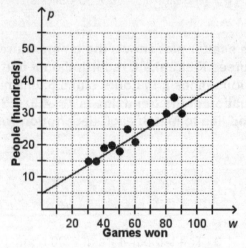

_____

_____

_____

_____

SELECTED RESPONSE
Select the correct answer.

1. In a poll, 150 students were asked if they prefer camping or going to the beach during their summer vacations and their gender. The data are shown in the two-way frequency table. What is the relative frequency of students who prefer going to the beach among all the students polled?

	Camping	Beach	Total
Boys	36	52	88
Girls	24	38	62
Total	60	90	150

(A) 25.3%

(B) 34.7%

(C) 40%

(D) 60%

2. In a poll, 200 people were asked if they prefer rock or country music. The length of their hair was also recorded. The data are shown in the two-way frequency table. Based on the table, which of the following statements is true?

	Rock	Country	Total
Short hair	75	50	125
Long hair	45	30	75
Total	120	80	200

(A) People who prefer country music are more likely to have long hair than those who prefer rock music.

(B) People who prefer country music are less likely to have long hair than those who prefer rock music.

(C) People who prefer rock music are as likely to have short hair as those who prefer country music.

(D) People who prefer rock music are more likely to have short hair than those who prefer country music.

3. In a poll, 100 people were asked to indicate if they prefer to drive a truck or a car and their gender. The data are shown in the two-way frequency table. Based on the table, which of the following statements is NOT true?

	Truck	Car	Total
Men	24	28	52
Women	12	36	48
Total	36	64	100

(A) Women are more likely to prefer driving cars than men.

(B) Men are less likely to prefer driving trucks than women.

(C) Women are less likely to prefer driving trucks than men.

(D) Men are less likely to prefer driving cars than women.

Select all correct answers.

4. Jordan asked 100 students at her school if they prefer cats or dogs. She also recorded their gender. The data are shown in the two-way frequency table. Based on the table, which of the following statements are true?

	Prefer cats	Prefer dogs	Total
Boys	8	38	46
Girls	24	30	54
Total	32	68	100

(A) Boys are less likely than girls to prefer cats.

(B) Girls are more likely than boys to prefer dogs.

(C) Boys are equally as likely as girls to prefer dogs.

(D) A student is more likely to prefer dogs to cats.

(E) A girl is more likely to prefer dogs to cats.

(F) A boy is more likely to prefer dogs to cats.

Name _____ Date_____ Class _____

CONSTRUCTED RESPONSE

5. In a poll, 200 computer users were asked if they prefer using a laptop computer or a desktop computer. Their age was also recorded. The data are shown in the two-way frequency table. How does age influence computer preference? Use relative frequencies to explain your answer.

	Laptop	Desktop	Total
40 years old or older	38	55	93
Under 40 years old	86	21	107
Total	124	76	200

_____

_____

6. In a poll, 100 people were asked if they prefer spring or fall and if they prefer summer or winter. The data are shown in the two-way frequency table. Is there an association between a preference for summer and a preference for fall? Use relative frequencies to explain your answer.

	Summer	Winter	Total
Spring	36	12	48
Fall	27	25	52
Total	63	37	100

_____

7. A poll of 200 voters in a community found that 30% are Democrats and 40% are independents. Of those who are Democrats, 40% are male. Of those who are Republicans, 60% are female. Of those who are independents, 60% are female.

   a. Make a two-way frequency table using the given information.

	Dem.	Rep.	Ind.	Total
Male				
Female				
Total				

b. Is there an association between gender and political party? Explain.

_____

_____

8. Edwin asked 150 students at his school if they prefer math or English classes. He also asked if they prefer fiction or nonfiction books. His results are shown in the two-way frequency table. Edwin wanted to know if there is an association between preferring nonfiction books and preferring math classes. His work is shown. Is Edwin correct? If so, explain. If not, identify the error and describe the correct association.

	Math	English	Total
Fiction	37	42	79
Nonfiction	49	22	71
Total	86	64	150

Relative frequency of students who prefer nonfiction books among all students polled:
$$\frac{71}{150} \approx 0.473 = 47.3\%$$
Relative frequency of students who prefer nonfiction books among those who prefer math classes:
$$\frac{49}{150} \approx 0.327 = 32.7\%$$
Since 47.3% > 32.7%, students who prefer math classes are less likely than the others to prefer nonfiction books.

_____

_____